# ILLUSIONS OF POWER

# ILLUSIONS OF POWER

## A History of the Washington Public Power Supply System (WPPSS)

# D. Victor Anderson

PRAEGER SPECIAL STUDIES • PRAEGER SCIENTIFIC

New York • Philadelphia • Eastbourne, UK
Toronto • Hong Kong • Tokyo • Sydney

**Library of Congress Cataloging in Publication Data**

Anderson, D. Victor.
  Illusions of power.

  Bibliography: p.
  Includes index.
  1. Washington Public Power Supply System.
  2. Electric utilities—Washington (State)    I. Title.
  HD9685.U7W343   1985       363.6'2'09797       84-18329
  ISBN 0-03-000369-5 (alk. paper)

HD
9685
.U7
W343
1985

Published in 1985 by Praeger Publishers
CBS Educational and Professional Publishing
a Division of CBS Inc.
521 Fifth Avenue, New York, NY 10175 USA

© 1985 by Praeger Publishers

56789 052 987654321

Printed in the United States of America
on acid-free paper

# PREFACE

This is the story of a crusade. It begins, as all crusades do, with virtuous, lion-hearted men leading armies that were poor in resources but mighty in spirit against a much more powerful, insidious foe. Hugely outgunned, the feisty public-power crusade nonetheless prevailed in the utility wars over the vast energy troves of the Pacific Northwest. Until a few years ago, the greatest triumph of the crusade was the Washington Public Power Supply System.

This history of WPPSS was written in the afterglow of the long struggle between private power companies and local public interests—a struggle now spent. In fact, this book was written from within an organization that combines the best efforts of both consumer-owned utilities and their investor-owned counterparts, working cooperatively to determine the energy future of the Northwest. It is a future ominously clouded by WPPSS. Therefore, these ten chapters might be called the power-planning perspective to the Supply System's past.

This is not intended to be an exposé, nor an exercise in finger pointing; much more heat than light has been shed on the subject of WPPSS by attempts to lay blame. It is hoped that new information offered here will assist readers in rethinking some of their opinions based on old preconceptions.

A great deal of material about the Supply System has been tied up in the courts by the lawsuits which even now are determining the fate of WPPSS. Many present employees of the agency and its constituent utilities, as well as those who worked for WPPSS in the past, declined to be interviewed for this book because their names are part of the litigation. Perhaps when the legal entanglements are all unraveled, a definitive account of what happened in the few years preceding the demise of Projects 4 and 5 will at last be unveiled. Until that day, I believe that this book will serve as the most comprehensive source for the truth about the Supply System.

# ACKNOWLEDGMENTS

For every person who could not offer me help in researching this subject, there were several whose services should not go unmentioned. Ken Billington graciously provided a wealth of experiences from his forty years as a public-power leader in Washington state; this book would have been impossible without his phenomenal memory and extraordinary insight.

My thanks are also extended to Richard Romanelli for going out of his way to give me valuable material, as well as allowing me a thorough tour of Satsop and the distinctly Northwestern community of Elma. Steve Irish and Rags Nowakowski offered similar kind assistance in Richland.

I am grateful to Hugh Houser for putting his confidence in me at the Pacific Northwest Utilities Conference Committee (PNUCC), where the idea for this book was born. Betsy Brown also took a chance on me in carrying "Illusions of Power" to acceptance at Praeger; I am indebted to her for those efforts, as well as those of Barbara Leffel, who has ably continued the work which Ms. Brown began.

Others who have contributed to this effort are Joan Whiley, Jim Perko, Jack Hare, Jack Welch, Gus Norwood, and Louise Kennedy. For their gracious services, acknowledgment is also made here to Scott and Christine McDanold, Barbara Freisen, Renee Boschero, and Brian Anderson. I especially thank my brother Greg for encouraging me to undertake this project and exhorting me onward when the way seemed long.

The unqualified support of my parents, John and Harriette Anderson, makes this book every bit as much theirs as it is mine. Their dedication has been unshakable throughout the months that brought this work to fruition; they will always be an inspiration to me.

Finally, I thank my wife Elizabeth for her patience and faith, which often sustained me during my introduction to the writer's life.

# ABBREVIATIONS

| | |
|---|---|
| AE | architect-engineer |
| AEC | Atomic Energy Commission |
| APPA | American Public Power Association |
| BPA | Bonneville Power Administration |
| DSI | direct-service industry |
| EFSEC | Energy Facility Siting Evaluation Committee (of the state of Washington) |
| EWEB | Eugene Water and Electric Board |
| FPC | Federal Power Commission |
| FTC | Federal Trade Commission |
| GAO | General Accounting Office |
| HGP | Hanford Generating Project |
| HTPP | Hydro-Thermal Power Program |
| IOU | investor-owned utility |
| IPCO | Idaho Power Company |
| JCAE | Joint Committee on Atomic Energy |
| JOA | joint operating agency |
| JPPC | Joint Power Planning Committee |
| MW | megawatt(s) |
| NELA | National Electric Light Association |
| NHCA | National Hells Canyon Association |
| NPR | new production reactor |
| NWPP | Northwest Power Pool |
| NWPPA | Northwest Public Power Association |
| NYPA | New York Power Authority |
| OMB | Office of Management and Budget |
| PGE | Portland General Electric Company |
| PNPC | Pacific Northwest Power Company |
| PNUCC | Pacific Northwest Utilities Conference Committee |
| PNWRPC | Pacific Northwest Regional Planning Commission |
| PPC | Public Power Council |
| PP&L | Pacific Power & Light Company |
| PSP&L | Puget Sound Power & Light Company |
| PUD | Public Utility District (Washington) or People's Utility District (Oregon) |

PWA        Public Works Administration
SCL        Seattle City Light
SEC        Securities and Exchange Commission
SPC        State Power Commission
TVA        Tennessee Valley Authority
WPPSS      Washington Public Power Supply System
WWP        Washington Water Power Company

## DEFINITIONS

activate.  In electric utility parlance, to be given the capacity of distributing electricity.

Atomic Energy Commission (AEC).  Federal agency overseeing construction and operation of nuclear power plants and production of nuclear weapons. Its regulatory functions over the nuclear industry were transferred in 1974 to the Nuclear Regulatory Commission.

Bonneville Power Administration.  See Appendix A.

direct-service industry (DSI).  One of 15 companies that purchase power directly from the Bonneville Power Administration. Seven are aluminum companies. The other nine produce a variety of other products including pulp and paper, chemicals, titanium, and nickel.

Hanford Generating Project (HGP).  A power plant at Hanford, Washington, which uses waste heat to produce steam for electricity generation from a reactor originally built to produce only plutonium (the N-reactor).

joint operating agency (JOA).  An organization formed by a group of business organizations to perform a particular function, using the pooled resources of the constituent entities.

Joint Committee on Atomic Energy (JCAE).  Government agency consisting of representatives from the House and Senate of the U.S. Congress, and from the scientific community. The JCAE proposes nuclear energy legislation to Congress.

megawatt (MW).  A unit of electrical energy. One MW is roughly equivalent to the amount of electricity required in meeting the energy needs of 200 average homes.

mill.  The equivalent of one-tenth of one cent, commonly used to express the cost of basic units of power, such as mills per kilowatt-hour.

net billing. A three-party transaction, wherein payments due one party are offset against payments due another party. In this case, the three parties are the Bonneville Power Administration, the owner of a power plant, and a BPA customer who as a participant in the plant has agreed to purchase a percentage of its output. Each month the customer pays the plant owner for the customer's share. The power, however, is assigned to BPA. BPA, in turn, credits the customer's bill for the amount the customer paid the owner. BPA then bills the customer for the balance, or net, of its BPA account. Net billing is currently used in financing Plants 1, 2, and 3 of the Washington Public Power Supply System.

Northwest Power Pool (NWPP). A group coordinating the operation of the region's power-producing capabilities. The NWPP was created in 1942 by order of the Defense Production Board for the purpose of coordinating the power output of all utilities in the region. The role of the NWPP was continued after the war; its major responsibilities include power production coordination, scheduling of maintenance outages, assisting with transmission system control, coordinating communication between members, and gathering data for planning.

Northwest Public Power Administration (NWPPA). A representative organization for publicly owned utilities, founded in 1941, with 140 members in nine states, British Columbia, and the Yukon Territory.

Pacific Northwest Utilities Conference Committee (PNUCC). A power planning organization comprising 19 public and four investor-owned utility members. PNUCC's policy committee represents 130 utilities and 15 direct-service industries, and is thus the only regionwide planning organization that includes all of BPA's wholesale customers.

PNUCC grew out of the Tacoma Conference of 1946 and was formally established under the Defense Electric Production Act of 1950. Its main function for many years was to combine the forecasts of power loads and resources of the region's utilities into a single West Group Forecast, which was published on an annual basis and projected ten years into the future. Since 1977, when it drafted a regional energy and conservation bill for the U.S. Congress, PNUCC has been playing an increasingly important role in power legislation and its attendant political discussion.

# CONTENTS

*Preface*                                                          *v*

*Acknowledgments*                                                *vii*

*Abbreviations*                                                   *ix*

1  Legacy of Two Power Magnates                                    1

2  Public Power Consolidates in Washington State                  21

3  The Partnership Policy                                         38

4  WPPSS: The First Years                                         48

5  The Juggernaut                                                 66

6  The Construction Program                                       79

7  Nuclear Boom Years                                             95

8  Out of Control                                                114

9  The Dream Crumbles                                            122

10  From Insult to Default                                       134

*Epilogue*                                                      *138*

*Bibliography*                                                  *139*

*Appendix A*                                                    *143*

*Appendix B*                                                    *145*

*Index*                                                         *154*

*About the Author*                                             *161*

# 1

# LEGACY OF TWO POWER MAGNATES

It was the greatest financial disaster of its kind in history.

Securities representing hundreds of millions of dollars in investments were declared worthless. Many of those millions had come from loans extended simply to finance interest on debt, which would never be repaid. Investors who, only a few months before, had bought into the utilities market on the promise of "no-risk guarantees of high returns" were left without hope of ever seeing their ventures come to fruition. Fast-talking stockbrokers were blamed. Lawsuits were launched. Government investigations were initiated. The total effect of it all was not immediately discernible, and even today—52 years later—the amount of hardship it ultimately caused can only be guessed. Of course, many shareholders who fell victim to the disaster had been well-to-do and savvy in the intricacies of high finance, and probably should have known better. But there were also many hundreds, perhaps thousands, of individuals owning stocks and bonds in the gigantic holding-company empire of Samuel Insull who were people of modest means: schoolteachers, farmers, laborers, retirees. They had bought into a byzantine corporate system which was as unfamiliar and perplexing to them as the labyrinth of Minos. But in the heady, easy-money days of the 1920s, proletarian speculation had at last become attainable on a mass scale, and the power in its attraction lay almost as much in its sheer novelty as in its potential for payoffs. And, for many years, there were payoffs; so, people had continued to buy pieces of the Insull pie. And the House of Insull continued to grow and diversify and consolidate until it rivaled even the House of Morgan.

1

Then, overextended, the mighty pyramid of holding companies collapsed like a house of cards. Federal investigators and creditors were left with the task of sifting through the ruins, while the old man who had started it all slipped away to Europe.

It was the summer of 1932.

Few people were more pleased with the daily news reports of the company-by-company dissolution of the Insull corporate holdings than Homer Bone. In the eyes of Bone and other public power advocates, Sam Insull and his ilk were the foremost enemies of the American people. Even from his hideout somewhere in Europe, Insull was a menace; it was not hard for Bone to imagine the crafty old former billionaire plotting his comeback after his fall into disgrace. Bone's allies in the national public-power movement agreed that the monopolist still presented a potential threat to their cause: If Insull were somehow to return to a position of power and prestige in a U.S. economy already exhausted and battered from the consequences of the driving greed that characterized his class, the result could be disastrous. So, candidate for U.S. Senator Homer T. Bone obliged many a handy podium with denunciations of the high price Americans were paying to finance the cupidity of Insull and of the private utilities in general, which Bone and his compatriots had for ten years been referring to as a single entity they called "the Power Trust."

Yet many of those who were sympathetic to his views advised Bone against becoming too strident when addressing the matter of Samuel Insull, at least until the former mogul had been returned to the United States and proven guilty of fraud, extortion, and a caseload of other felonies of which he was accused. The economic depression that most Americans were enduring was still too young for them to have lost faith in capitalism, Bone's friends cautioned. And Insull had been known for years as the capitalist's capitalist.

The success story of Samuel Insull was so uniquely American in its Horatio Algeresque exposition that practically every redblooded schoolboy knew and coveted it. Born in the slums of London, Insull sailed to New York at the age of 19 in 1881, the year that Thomas Alva Edison designed the world's first electrical generating station. Insull had, in fact, come to the United States at the invitation of the Wizard of Menlo Park himself, who had heard of the young Englishman's quick intelligence from Edison's London representative. In spite of having no more than the equivalent of a high school education, young Sam assisted the famed genius in building that pioneer power station on Pearl Street in Manhattan. Insull became Edison's private secretary and, in a few years, his most trusted advisor. One day, Edison told Insull to go up to Schenectady and run one of his General Electric outfits that had been steadily losing money for years. "Whatever you do, Sam," the inventor had told him, "either make a brilliant success of it or a brilliant failure. Do something!" Insull did something. In less than ten years, he turned an operation of 200 men into Schenectady's biggest and most successful employer, with Insull in charge of the whole work force of 6,000. In 1892, he was sent to Chicago to head the infant Chicago Edison. He first bought a portion of shares in the company so that he would be the major stockholder. The next year, he convinced the rival Commonwealth Electric Company that the two Chicago utilities could grow faster and make more money if they stopped competing against each other and let him run both. He was promptly made president of Commonwealth and, in 1907, consolidated both utilities as Commonwealth Edison.

Thus began the pattern that would typify the Englishman's financial flair and become a national mania for big business during the 1920s. He began buying small electric companies in the area around Chicago, combining them into the Public Service Company of Northern Illinois. Next, he took over the nearly bankrupt Peoples Gas, Light & Coke Company. He formed a separate By-Products Corporation, financed by sale of Peoples Gas stock, then proceeded to sell gas to the parent company cheaper than before. Eventually, he combined Commonwealth Edison, Public Service of Northern Illinois, and Peoples Gas into a giant holding company: the Middle West Utilities Company. Middle West was, in turn, controlled by Insull Utility Investments, Inc., the sole function of which was to buy and sell securities. And even beyond this company was the Corporation Securities Company of Chicago, a "super holding company" called "Corps" for short. Corps controlled Insull Utility by owning 30 percent of its stock. Yet Insull Utility also held 12.5 percent of Corps stock, a controlling interest, and another 1.2 percent of Corps stock was held by Middle West. One financial observer of this structure, commenting on the term parent company being given to entities in the framework, despaired: "In what sort of family is the child a grandparent of the father?"

Naturally, the whole complicated process (known as pyramiding) caught on fast in the business world of the 1920s; it could not have happened sooner. It had to await a vast congregation of speculators, or at least investors. The congregation developed in no small part because the years of World War I had created, through Liberty bonds, a whole new class of investors, people who had never before owned a bond or a share of stock in anything. Encouraging speculation in the enormous amounts of new paper generated by the holding companies was the very liberal credit allowed by reputable banks to margin purchasers of questionable securities or of reliable securities at questionable prices. But Americans in the 1920s seemed as willing to buy any stock, just as they'd try a swig from any bottle plainly labeled whiskey. U.S. business, so the prophets cried in the marketplace, was headed for new frontiers, carrying with it to affluence all who possessed the wit to buy shares—shares in anything offered by these new and generous masters of capital who were inviting the man in the street, and even the streetsweeper, along with the barber, the storeclerk, and the housewife to join them in the golden opportunity.

From atop the pyramid of power he had built almost single-handedly, Samuel Insull by 1925 controlled a vast empire of utilities serving 2 million customers in 39 states. His immediate domain was Chicago, where he rode through the streets in a 16-cylinder Cadillac that was armor plated from radiator cap to rear bumper and had windows of plate glass an inch thick. He was accompanied around the clock by a dozen armed bodyguards. The guards and the bullet-proof car were part of the price one paid for possessing clout in Al Capone's town, and Insull had plenty of clout. He and his colleagues were always ready to aid whatever party was in power. A local newspaperman said it was worth a million dollars to any man to be seen chatting with Sam Insull in front of the Continental Bank. Utilities executives around the country referred to Chicago as "Insullopolis."

Cracks began to appear in the Insull pyramid in 1926, when bears in the utilities market caused prices of stocks in Insull's holding companies to drop sharply. The companies within the Insull network frantically bought into each other until the face value of their shares was restored to previous levels, and the financial damage was contained. The following year, the entire electrical utilities industry received a shock that would have more far-reaching consequences: The Federal Trade Commission (FTC) began an investigation of public relations information practices of power companies. The focus of the investigation was the National Electric Light Association (NELA), a "trade organization" founded by Martin Insull, president of Middle West Utilities and Samuel's brother.

The FTC inquiry was to last nearly ten years, and each year's passing seemed to mark a more odious aspect of the business community revealed. NELA, the Commission was to discover, was little more than a propaganda vehicle for the private power utilities, with virtually unlimited access to funds. Along with blatant abuses of the truth in its all-media advertising, NELA engaged in setting up and subsidizing front groups with names such as "Citizens' Committee" and "Taxpayers' Association," whose sole, covert function was to represent private power's interests in local elections and initiatives. It seemed that the utilities were not satisfied with monopolizing the electrical industry, but felt compelled to maintain control over public opinion as well. The bulk of NELA's considerable resources was thrown into the growing debate over public power, which went back to the dawn of the Electric Age.

Even before Edison and Insull had ushered in that age with the first power station on Pearl Street, the question arose as to whether investors or consumers should own the means of generating and distributing electricity. Prior to the 1920s, with most transmission networks securely in the grasp of the investor-owned companies, the private-versus-public issue had been confined to a few localized rivalries. But a handful of Progressivist politicians-most notably Senator George W. Norris of Nebraska and Governor Gifford Pinchot of Pennsylvania —sought out potential arenas for jousts against the monolith of the Power Trust. Their efforts had, by the beginning of the 1920s, broadened the scope of the power debate to national dimensions. In 1922, Norris introduced a bill in the Senate that would create a federal corporation to operate government-owned power facilities on the Tennessee River at Muscle Shoals, Alabama. The bill was a countermove against Henry Ford's intention to purchase the facilities from the government and build more dams in the Tennessee Valley, all for the use of private enterprise. The nation's private utilities, sensing that Norris's measure could take the hydroelectric potential of most of the South out of their hands forever, mounted a public relations blitz against public power and redoubled their lobbying efforts on Capitol Hill. The battle for Muscle Shoals lasted 11 years and served as the focal point for the national power fight before it was finally decided from the White House.

The tactics used by NELA to block a government takeover of Muscle Shoals were often insidious, as the FTC was to discover. Newspaper editors across the country were bombarded with letters, supposedly written by average citizens, which attacked the Norris bill as a "sabotage of free enterprise" and a "Bolshevik plot." Many of these letters were traced by the FTC to the Salem, Oregon offices of E.F. Hofer & Sons, where a paid staff worked full time cranking out the misbegotten missives at the behest and expense of NELA.

It was known that the Insull brothers were key financial contributors to NELA, and were widely assumed that the organization reflected their views on the power controversy. But threading a clear line of responsibility through the maze of Insull's companies was deemed by the FTC to be difficult, if not impossible, and no attempt was made to investigate. Judge Robert Healy, the Commission's counsel, concluded: "I do not believe that the human being has ever lived who could know enough to run that whole Insull outfit."

Still, the endless allegations did not lead to a popular outcry against the Insulls at that time, which is understandable. After all, the brothers appeared to be running an efficient (albeit confusing) business, and their occasional lapses into media manipulation didn't seem to be hurting anyone. Despite pleas from the public-power movement, few politicians dared suggest a government investigation of Samuel Insull's corporate affairs while he remained so successful. Even the Great Crash of the stock market merely underscored his apparent invincibility. Ten days after Black Thursday in October of 1929, Insull opened the palatial, $20 million Civic Opera House in Chicago, his gift to the city inspired by his love of opera. Confident that this depression would be no worse than those he had weathered in the past, he quickened the pace of his investment decisions. He began construction of a Texas-to-Chicago natural gas pipeline, set out to rehabilitate the textile and shipbuilding industries of New England, and single-handedly rescued the city of Chicago from bankruptcy by paying off its debt of over $50 million. As the Depression deepened, he took on greater and greater financial burdens until it appeared as if he were attempting to carry the entire U.S. economy on his shoulders. For the next two years, the Insull companies were able to stay solvent through the kind of bookkeeping sleight-of-hand that had carried them through the rough months of 1926. But the legerdemain could not go on forever, and as months of accumulating red ink turned into years, the order went down the steps of the Insull pyramid from the oldest vice-president to the newest office boy: Sell stock if you want to hold on to your job. Uncles, aunts, and cousins heeded anxious pleas from Insull employees, scraping crumpled dollars out of cracked teapots and sugarbowls. As Insull's fortune disappeared into the drain of corporate debt, it sucked thousands of others down with it.

In April of 1932, Middle West went into receivership. One by one, the 95 holding companies and 255 operating companies in the sprawling Insull empire failed. Having lost the shield of legitimate power that success and money had afforded him, Sam Insull fled to France.

The news of Insull's spectacular fall from grace was of particular interest to Americans in the torpid summer of 1932: first, because it offered cathertic relief from the depressing reports of growing soup lines and drought-stricken farmers scoured with dust; second, because it was an election year, and the crippling of private utilities had rendered them newly vulnerable in the debate over public power. With respect to the power issue, the object of speculation was the Democratic presidential nominee, Governor Franklin Delano Roosevelt of New York.

President Herbert Hoover, the Republican incumbent, was a known quantity, having made his position clear by a controversial veto of Norris's Muscle Shoals bill. Although Roosevelt had not made a public pronouncement on Muscle Shoals, public-power advocates were heartened when he established the New York Power Authority (NYPA), a state agency created for the purpose of developing electrical generating operations on the St. Lawrence River, with the resulting power designated for private enterprise. Political insiders spoke of FDR's firm belief in more government regulation of private utilities, but his views on the more volatile issue of public ownership were largely unknown. As late as September of 1932, the path of the Democratic candidate remained to be charted. That month, the Roosevelt entourage arrived in the Pacific Northwest, where it was widely expected FDR would give his long-awaited stand on public power.

The Northwest was a fitting place for Roosevelt to announce his presidential power policy. The region possessed 40 percent of the nation's potential hydroelectric power. The Columbia River, with only a few small dams on its 150 tributaries, contained the mightiest power sources on the North American continent. Its development represented the key to future economic growth for that far corner of the United States. Spokesmen from the area had striven throughout the 1920s to obtain federal dams on the Columbia, but to no avail. Naturally, the struggle for control of the Northwest's vast energy resources had been a long and bitter one between public and private interests. For that reason, Roosevelt knew as he arrived in Seattle that his audiences in the region were already familiar with the symbols and nuances of the power fight. And he had received a briefing on the regional situation before leaving New York from a man who for many years had been at the eye of the political storm over the future of Northwest power: J.D. Ross.

In 1932, the name of James Delmadge Ross was practically synonymous with public power in the Northwest. Having emerged triumphant from a dramatic attempt to unseat him as head of the nation's largest publicly owned utility, Ross's fame had attained national proportions. It was ironic that the transplanted Canadian, having been fired by the mayor of Seattle, had gone straight to work for the governor of New York and then, almost overnight, had become a confidant of the presidential nominee. But J.D. Ross was used to odd twists of fate. Like Samuel Insull, he was an immigrant who had arrived in the United States young and penniless, eventually to find fame and fortune as a leader in the power industry. However, the similarities between the utility bosses end there, for in the course of their lives they were to blaze trails to opposite poles of the electrical business.

Born in Chatham, Ontario, in 1871, Ross displayed an early fascination with science. In 1881, while Edison was designing the Pearl Street Station and young Insull was crossing the Atlantic for the first time, ten-year-old J.D. built his first working electric battery out of a strip of zinc and an old copper kettle filled with pickle juice. As a boy, Ross tinkered tirelessly in his homemade laboratory, dabbling in experiments with photography, explosives, and radio waves. Later, he took enough college-level courses to obtain a teacher's certificate, then went to work as an instructor in the local school. In 1897, Ross was diagnosed for tuberculosis, the same disease that had killed his mother when he was seven. In defiance of his doctor's orders, the young schoolteacher quit the classroom to join the great Yukon gold rush. He told his brother before he left that, if he were destined to die young, he would do it on the road to adventure and fortune. His doctor predicted that Ross would not come back alive.

After a year of prospecting in the harsh frontier of the Artic wilderness, Ross secured something more precious than gold nuggets—his health. He made his way south to the west coast, arriving in Seattle at the turn of the century. His proclivity with electricity landed him a job with the fledgling, municipally owned electric system. Within ten years, the dynamic Canadian was put in charge of Seattle City Light as its superintendant. He built a powerhouse on the Cedar River to deliver electricity over a high-voltage transmission line 37 miles long—an unprecedented distance. He designed and constructed a distribution network for Seattle that was second only to Insull's "systematization" grid in Chicago; Seattle's electric rates, meanwhile, were one-fifth those of Insullopolis. Even lower than Seattle's rates were those of the neighboring municipal light system of the city of Tacoma, whose ratepayers enjoyed the lowest electric bills in the nation. In 1922, the two utilities installed the world's first publicly owned intermunicipal tie line, interconnecting the two public power systems. The efficiency and thrift of the Washington municipals were a constant embarrassment to the country's private monopolies.

City Light's rival for the Seattle market was Puget Sound Power & Light (PSP&L), owned by the Stone & Webster holding company of Boston. Ross's attempts to purchase prime hydroelectric development sites on the Skagit River northeast of Seattle were blocked by PSP&L, which owned the sites. Ross appealed to the federal government, pointing out that Puget was buying up other sites without first developing the ones it held on the Skagit. When the government decided in Ross's favor and turned the entire river over to City Light, public power supporters everywhere hailed it as a coup. Interestingly, a public relations gimmick had Seattle's power from the Skagit activated for the first time in 1924 from a switch in West Orange, New Jersey, flipped by Sam Insull's old boss, Thomas Edison.

Ross's victory in seizing the Skagit incurred the wrath of the Power Trust, and from that day it sought to destroy his credibility as an outspoken, public-spirited visionary. Its methods ranged from setting up dummy ratepayer organizations in Seattle to discredit Ross as a socialist, to the bugging of Ross's home with a dictaphone planted inside his chimney. One after another, corporation executives were sent from Boston to manage the competing PSP&L to a position of dominance over City Light, but to no avail. J.D. Ross, in spite of his reputation as a genius, was a small-town man in personality, inspiring confidence in the people of his community. A bear of a man with huge head and hands, he nonetheless seemed harmless; his favorite hobbies were birdwatching and gardening. His placid look, slow gait, and rumpled blue serge suits with shiny knees and elbows belied the quick, politically astute mind within.

The Power Trust continually underestimated Ross, as well as the forces he could muster when confronted with a challenge. One of his biggest challenges was trying to expand City Light's service to outlying suburbs which had been asking for power from Puget; it seemed to ignore them. Washington state law prohibited municipals from selling electricity outside city limits. Ross was reduced to frustration as communities outside of Seattle which were lucky enough to finally receive service from PSP&L nonetheless paid up to four times the rate of Seattle power users, while City Light burgeoned with power surpluses. But Ross found a key ally in his effort to change the state law in the public's favor: a young legislator by the name of Homer Truitt Bone.

At about the time that Ross was first settling in Seattle, Homer T. Bone arrived in Tacoma from Indiana. His idealism showed from the outset of his career. He became a lawyer, fought for liberalization of labor laws, and ran for local office on the Socialist ticket. Unsuccessful in his first bid for election, he switched to the more moderate Farmer-Labor party and won a seat in the Washington legislature in 1922. As a resident of Tacoma and representative of farmers' interests, it was natural that Bone was drawn into the power issue. He saw the injustice of private companies which required that the farmer pay the cost of rural service extensions. By aiding farm mutual electric companies or cooperatives in organizing to tap municipal lines just inside Tacoma's city limits, he played a key role in bringing the first public rural electrification to Washington. But the process was piecemeal; what was needed was legislation that would allow cities to sell power outside of their boundaries. When such a measure was introduced by Bone in the legislature in 1924, it marked the first time that the populist device of the initiative was used in Washington. If the initiative (called the Bone Bill) were successful, the door was open to the municipalities to link up on a broad scale with the farmers. This was an advance that the private utilities viewed with foreboding, and they opened up with all the weapons at their disposal. Years later, the FTC probe ascertained that an expenditure of at least $175,000 in advertising and publicity costs was used by NELA to blast the Bone Bill. Some newspapermen more familiar with such costs estimated that the figure was closer to a million. Meanwhile, the public power supporters worked on a shoestring, and Bone himself wound up with a $6,000 mortgage on his home. The Bone Bill went down to defeat, and its namesake reflected on his feelings of bitterness when he later wrote: "I was held up to ridicule and scorn in every corner of the state and emerged a ruined man." Stung by the costliness of his loss, Bone quit politics at the end of his term and went to work as an attorney for the port of Tacoma.

But the revelations of the Power Trust's propagandist methods which emerged from the FTC hearings, combined with the urgings of his compatriots in the public-power movement, worked to restore

Bone's appetite for the fray. The onset of the Depression had caused a change in the mood of the people of the Northwest in 1930. Bone and his friend George Joseph in Oregon detected that the atmosphere was ripe for political risk taking. So, the two men drafted the Northwest's first Public Utility District (PUD) laws, and succeeded in having the laws placed on the ballots for the fall elections in Washington and Oregon. The PUD laws enabled a county or a part of a county to organize itself into a centralized utility for its area, called a public utility district in Washington and a people's utility district in Oregon. The PUD unashamedly borrows a rule from page one of the private utilities' economic textbook: The business advantages of a monopoly are improved efficiency, increased assets, and reduced capital risks. From a consumer viewpoint, the resulting benefits are lower rates and better service. Small, scattered municipal systems could, under the PUD law, join together to gain the advantages of interconnection and load integration, and at the same time bring service to rural areas between. In effect, the PUD combined rural electrification and municipal ownership. Hitherto, farmers had witnessed the lowering of rates with municipal ownership, but were without the legal institutional framework for achieving the same for themselves. Small wonder, then, that the Grange organizations of states were the primary sponsors of the measures.

The PUD was not a new idea in 1930. Nebraska's electrical needs were completely served by publicly owned utilities called public-power districts, a situation due in large part to the efforts of the state's native son George Norris. But the great majority of the country was electrified by private companies, if it was electrified at all. The vast rural areas of the United States were, for the most part, still in darkness simply because distribution to farms was not profitable for investor-owned utilities. In the Pacific Northwest, the McMinnville PUD in Oregon had supplied some of the region's first electricity in the 1880s, but it had formed before the laws were changed, limiting public power to the city limits of municipalities. Bone, Joseph, and the Granges were determined to change the laws again.

In spite of the usual strong opposition from the Power Trust, the PUD law campaigns were successful in both states. Indicative of the shift in public attitudes brought on by the Depression is the fact that the implications of the PUD laws were far more sweeping than those of the Bone Bill which had failed four years before.

Triumphant at last, Bone was courted by both major political parties, which aspired to run him for national office. Hoover's anti-public-power stance made the choice easy for Bone: He obtained the Democratic nomination for the U.S. Senate in 1932.

Bone's was not the only political stock on the rise within the ranks of the public-power movement. For J.D. Ross, the events that would lead to his being catapulted into the inner circle of the president himself began shortly after the elections in the fall of 1930. Mayor Frank Edwards of Seattle made a trip back east and, while in Boston, visited the offices of the Stone & Webster Corporation. What he discussed with the people there is not known, but letters written later to the president of Puget Sound Power & Light from his boss at Stone & Webster indicate that Edwards was treated magnanimously by the company's top executives. A few months later, on March 9, 1931, Edwards fired J.D. Ross, who had served 30 years at City Light, 20 of them as superintendant.

Pandemonium broke out in Seattle. Civic groups across the city immediately demanded an explanation. Ross's supporters insisted that Edwards be recalled. The Seattle *Post-Intelligencer* headline the morning of March 10 blazed: "MAYOR OUSTS ROSS: FACES RECALL." Before a grim city council, Edwards defended his action: "The influence of Communism in this [City Light] department must be stamped out. . . ." Across the country in Albany, New York, Morris Cooke (trustee of the newly formed New York Power Authority) read the news from Seattle with interest. Later, Cooke invited Ross to serve as a consultant to the NYPA on marketing power from the St. Lawrence River. Ross spent a month in New York, and in the course of his consulting work, became acquainted with Governor Roosevelt. The two men took an immediate liking to each other, sharing a taste for the risk and challenge of experimentation in projects and policies. When Ross returned to Seattle to a huge reception by his supporters, Roosevelt wrote to congratulate him on his ability to inspire such loyalty in his community. Shortly after, Edwards was ousted as mayor, and the new mayor restored Ross to his post at the head of City Light, an event that made headlines around the United States. If there had been complicity by the Power Trust at the beginning of this string of occurrences, it had backfired spectacularly.

But the ascendancy of the leaders of the public-power movement in Washington was a mixed blessing. Bone's nomination for the Senate had caused a split in the Democratic ranks between "standpatters" who were upset over Bone's socialist background, and liberals who refused to endorse anyone else. The disunity threatened to undermine the entire Democratic campaign in the state, right up to the time when FDR himself arrived in Seattle in September 1932. The Roosevelt campaign train stopped at a country crossroads just outside the city, where a motorcade into Seattle was to begin. Realizing that even an appearance with Bone could hurt FDR's chances of winning the state of Washington, Ross secretly spirited out Bone to the remote intersection, where the three men talked over the situation in Roosevelt's car. FDR declared that, much as he wanted to win it, he could probably afford to lose Washington in the election and still win the presidency, whereas Bone could not afford such a loss. The men agreed that FDR's endorsement of Bone might do some harm to the presidential nominee, but that it would help Bone's candidacy a great deal. It was decided that Roosevelt would announce his support for Bone that day.

Aside from enthusiastic praise for Homer Bone, FDR's Seattle speech stayed away from the issue of public power. But at his next campaign stop, in Portland, Roosevelt spelled out the fundamentals of his power policy for the first time. He began the address to his Oregon audience by affirming that he shared the belief of most Americans that electric rates were too high. In order to remedy this situation, he called for more regulation, on federal and state levels, of utilities and holding companies. He advocated the application of prudential investment theory to valuation and full publicity of capital issues of stocks, bonds, and securities. On the subject of public ownership, Roosevelt stated categorically that "as a broad general rule the development of utilities should remain, with certain exceptions, a function for private initiative and private capital." He held that a city or district should have the right to go into the electrical business, but he did not consider that it would take that step if provided with adequate service at reasonable rates. Public ownership at the local level was the "last resort" if all else failed. As for government ownership and operation, Roosevelt maintained that power sites owned by the states or federal government should be developed by the commonwealth but that ". . .private capital should. . .be given the first opportunity to transmit and distribute the power." He envisioned four great federal power developments: the St. Lawrence River in the Northeast, Muscle Shoals in the Southeast, Boulder Dam in the Southwest, and the Columbia River in the Northwest. Each of these would provide a national "yardstick": a range of standard rates to compare against existing rates. The result, Roosevelt said, would be a "new deal. . .between the electric utilities on the one side, and the consumer and investor on the other."

FDR employed two key symbols in his Portland speech which manifested and characterized the tension in the country at that time.

One was the name of Insull, which Roosevelt used to invoke the "spectre of the private utility past." He referred to the "Insull monstrosity" as having done more to open the eyes of the U.S. public to the truth than anything else. In Roosevelt's words, "the public paid and paid dearly" for such financial manipulations as Insull practiced. He asked his audience to judge him by the enemies he had made: "Judge me by the selfish purposes of these utility leaders who have talked of radicalism while they were selling watered stock to the people. . . ." FDR's diatribe should have suprised no one. After all, his address had been written by campaign speechwriter Harold Ickes, who was an old Insull nemesis from his days as a Chicago newspaper columnist. And, hiding out across the Atlantic, Insull no longer possessed an aura of justified acheivement. Two things were apparent from FDR's choice of the Insull tropology: first, the Democratic candidate was solidly in the anti-Power Trust camp; and second, Insull, even in his absence from the U.S. scene, was still a powerful symbol, but of power in the past.

The other symbol that Roosevelt used in his speech represented power for the future, power to be wielded by the people, but actually to be implemented only when necessary. This talisman was a "birch rod in the cupboard to be taken out and used only when the child gets beyond the point where a mere scolding does no good." The imagery evoked by the combination of these symbols—the right of the people to operate their own utility, seen as a birch rod which by its silent presence cows the naughty child representing the Power Trust—formed an effective picture in the minds of those who were not convinced that government- or consumer-owned power was the answer to the excesses of investor-owned utilities. A regulatory birch rod was a more appealing picture to most Americans, compared to a public-power mallet breaking the private monopolies to pieces.

Public-power advocates in the Northwest were disappointed with what they perceived as a compromising stance in FDR's power policy, though they realized that it was politically expedient for him to do so. Therefore, celebration among the public-power crowd was low-key when Roosevelt won the presidency that November. They saw him as a national figure with unusual sympathies toward their cause, but they were well acquainted with the kind of odds he was up against. Even Bone's simultaneous ascendancy to the Senate was viewed by those in the public-power movement as a step toward a larger goal, instead of an end in itself. Senator Bone himself was not content to rest on his laurels; he and Ross were convinced that the Northwest power war would not be won until every private utility in the region was purchased by the PUDs and municipals, right down to the last substation. It would take time; the proposed Columbia River dams provided by the New Deal were a start, but the public-power movement was under no illusions—the road ahead would be long and difficult, even with the sanction rendered by a public-minded administration. But Bone, Ross, Joseph and others had staked too much on the cause to give up. In the course of their battles with the Power Trust, they had become familiar with the ways of their enemy. The deceitful propaganda, the insensitivity to consumers' needs, the invasions of personal privacy—all that the public-power leaders had experienced first-hand at the propagation of the private utilities—gave men such as Ross and Bone a conviction of the righteousness of their cause. In their minds, the cause had become a crusade for public power; literally, a struggle between good and evil. Bone in particular nourished an abiding hatred for the private companies that went back to the humiliation he suffered at the hands of NELA in 1924. Years later, in 1939, he still harbored a distrust that bordered on paranoia, as shown in a letter to Washington voters, in which he compared the campaign against his Bone Bill to the methods employed in Hitler's Germany:

> This was done in pursuance of a plan originated by the notorious Insulls of Illinois. The scheme was worthy of the sinister brain of the Nazi Goebbels. Like the Nazi propagandist, the utilities adopted lying as a propaganda weapon. The basic Insull strategy, as used in our State was—and I quote the authors: "...Logic won't work...so use lies instead...." That was the utility policy, and still is.

The height of private power's hubris, in the eyes of the public power crusaders, was its unrestrained sales of mountainous amounts of securities to ordinary citizens unwise to the ins and outs of the markets. At a hearing on Muscle Shoals at which he testified shortly after being sworn in as Senator, Bone put forward the crusader view:

> These companies simply sold the people counterfeits; the "prior preference," "pluperfect," "superheterodyne" stock they unloaded was counterfeit. Insull's graft is a fine example. . . . I say that these big fellows have gone unwhipped, while they were unloading billions of dollars of worthless trash on the country.

Although not as grandiloquent as his compatriot in the Senate, Ross expressed a concurrence with Bone in the matter of the holding company debacle when, in responding to the private utilities' objection to federal ownership of dams, he observed, "It will be remembered, and very bitterly, that these same private power people did not howl or worry when they sold a lot of worthless securities to an unsuspecting public and brought the collapse out of which the President is now leading us." In 1933, the United States turned to the president for leadership out of the collapse, and for justice done to those who caused it. The name at the top of most people's lists was Insull.

During his campaign, Roosevelt had never actually specified his intentions in the matter of bringing Samuel Insull home to answer charges, but he must have felt obligated by the many allegations he had fired at the former monopolist in the heat of the presidential race. Throughout 1933, U.S. authorities demanded that the Greek government extradite Insull. It was known that Insull had gone from Paris to Greece at the invitation of Basil Zaharoff, the notorious and fabulously wealthy arms merchant and long-time crony of Insull. Finally, at year's end, the U.S. State Department exerted economic pressure on Athens to surrender the fugitive. Greece still refused, but ordered Insull to leave. The old man chartered an aromatic Greek tramp steamer and drifted around the eastern Mediterranean for two weeks, sending requests to the governments of Egypt, Turkey, and Rumania to grant him asylum. At last he landed in Turkey, where he was promptly put into jail. U.S. officials arrived to put him on a ship for the long sail to New York.

Back in Washington, D.C., federal investigators were sifting through mountains of records and documents seized from the 350 companies that Samuel and Martin Insull had left as their legacy. They discovered that, even in its glory, the crumbling pyramid had consisted mostly of paper. The investment which the Insulls had made to secure the direction of the entire network of corporations was something less than a million dollars. At the peak of the Insulls' power in March of 1930, the market value of the actual Insull investment amounted to $100 million. That $100 million, however, controlled $2.5 billion. For every dollar that the Insulls originally invested, they controlled $2,500 of the public's money. Watching the investigations of the Senate Committee on Banking and Commerce as it unraveled the corporate tangle of companies and investments, author Frederick Lewis Allen wrote:

> To look at a chart of the Insull pyramid as it appeared during those lush days is almost to be persuaded that one is dreaming. Certainly, one thinks, here is corporate capitalism gone mad.

He added, "Pyramiding. . .took inordinate profits out of the consumer, the investor, and the future—often including of course the insiders' own future, as Samuel Insull subsequently discovered." Owen D. Young, chairman of the board of General Electric, testified before the committee regarding Insull's operations. He confessed to a feeling of helplessness when he began examining the complicated structure of holding companies and "investment" companies superimposed atop one another. It was, said Young, "impossible for any man, however able, really to grasp the situation." In Young's opinion, Sam Insull became a victim of the monster system he had created and "which got even beyond his power, competent as he was, to understand it."

Insull arrived at the Cook County jail in Chicago in April, 1934. His attorney came offering to post bail, but the old Englishman refused it. He spent a night in a cell with assorted criminals, including a murderer, before a judge ordered him moved to a private hospital cell.

A year later, a failing toy and hobby company named Parker Brothers released "Monopoly," a board game that featured a cartoon monopolist on all the game's "Chance" and "Community Chest" cards. The character, a plump man sporting a sweeping white mustache, decked out in top hat and tails, seemed vaguely familiar to the thousands who were to buy the first edition of the game, particularly when he was depicted standing outside an opera house. But it was the card that portrayed the little old man in the clutches of a cop, billy club raised over bald head, that gave the caricature away. The card read:

GO TO JAIL
GO DIRECTLY TO JAIL
DO NOT PASS GO
DO NOT COLLECT $200

Samuel and Martin Insull were charged with mail fraud, embezzlement on state and federal levels, and federal violation of the Bankruptcy Act. Throughout 1934 and half of 1935, the trials went on in Illinois and U.S. courts, and at the end of each case, right to the last, the verdict was the same: acquitted on all counts.

Sam Insull spent most of the rest of his life in Paris, living quietly off of the generous pension which had been restored to him following his final acquittal. He did not live long enough to attend the Chicago World's Fair of 1939, which he had conceived in the early days of 1932 as a way to counter the effects of the Depression in Insullopolis.

As a direct result of the Senate probe into Insull's ruined enterprise, Congress passed the Public Utility Holding Company Act of 1935. In conjunction with the act, the Securities and Exchange Commission (SEC) was formed to decide which of the nation's holding companies should be allowed to stay in business. Roosevelt called Ross to the White House in August to ask him to serve as a member of the SEC. The president told J.D. that he was the best man in the country for the position, and that the SEC's work would tie in with the consulting that Ross was doing for the new Federal Power Commission (FPC). Ross accepted and took a leave of absence from his Seattle City Light post. However, from the beginning it was clear that FDR had made a mistake. Ickes, who had been elevated from campaign speechwriter to Secretary of the Interior, noted that Ross was out of his "line" at the SEC and was "more or less a misfit." Justice William O. Douglas, who served on the Commission with his fellow Washingtonian Ross, recalled that "J.D. Ross had a very fine relationship with the Members of the Commission. Everybody liked him. He had, however, a one-track mind—namely, public power. And he had very little interest in the other manifold aspects of the Commission's work." Ross was bewildered by the financial maze that characterized the holding companies, and knew next to nothing of bonds and securities; after all, he was first an engineer—a veritable genius in the physical sciences who was known as one of a handful of men who could comprehend Einstein's theory of relativity. But the securities business was not a science; this was corporate voodoo, fiscal prestidigitation. Ross had always let someone else at City Light handle the economic side of his engineering marvels. The SEC work was the only project taken on by J.D. Ross from which he backed away without a fight. Not long after his appointment to the Commission, Ross wrote the president to ask for another assignment. In a way, even in its shattered state, the Power Trust had overwhelmed the old public power magnate.

Yet, in finding himself unable to serve his nation in one capacity, Ross found once again that he could do a much greater work for the Pacific Northwest. He joined an intensive planning effort being coordinated by the Pacific Northwest Regional Planning Commission (PNWRPC) under the auspices of the Federal Emergency Administration of Public Works (PWA). The purpose of the effort was to come up with a comprehensive plan for marketing and distributing power from the two huge federal dams under construction on the Columbia River, one at Grand Coulee (in the arid central portion of Washington which is part of that tableland covering two-thirds of the state and known as Eastern Washington), the other on that portion of the river forming a border between Oregon and Washington. Portland had already "claimed" this latter project, arguing that power from the future dam should be sold directly to Portland utilities, which were in the "best" position to transmit the electricity on to other Oregon communities. Eastern Washington residents likewise viewed Grand Coulee as theirs, vowing that no power from the proposed dam would go over the Cascade Mountains until they had first satisfied all of their electrical needs. This chagrined western Washingtonians on the other side of the Cascades, who were harder hit by unemployment than their eastern neighbors, and believed that they were thus justified in having at least equal access to Grand Coulee's power.

The reports to the PNWRPC, for the most part, admonished this tendency toward provincialism. They emphasized a broad, regional approach to the problem. They pointed out that, long before electric power ever became an issue, the people of the Pacific Northwest had already developed a unique sense of "place," a considerable regional consciousness, due to the region's situation as a rather distinct geographic and economic entity, and to its common historical background, its economic ties, and its cultural homogeneity. These factors had brought a unity to the region which transcended the natural diversities of its land and its people who made their living off that land: Whether it was lumbermen in damp rain forests, herdsmen on dusty plains, fishermen off misty coasts, shepherds in high deserts, farmers in fertile valleys, wardens in snowy mountain parks, or workmen on the projects that would tame the great rivers, all were knit together in a common destiny based on common interests and needs distinct from those of the rest of the nation. This common destiny, stated the final report of the PNWRPC, had outgrown the boundaries of the states of Washington and Oregon (and indeed the geographical parameters of the Pacific Northwest, as well defined as they are, were of course never perceived in terms of discrete political entities) and thus comprised all of Idaho, that portion of Montana lying west of the Rocky Mountains, and bits of Wyoming, Utah, Nevada, and California. The threads tying this vast (300,000 square miles) area together are the Columbia and its tributaries, notably the Snake and Willamette Rivers, which form the region's central physical feature, the Columbia Basin. The development of the basin's resources, concluded the PNWRPC, would require a single federal agency with a scope and perspective that would override local interests and continue the tradition of regionalism which had blessed the people of the Northwest with an extraordinary sense of identity and purpose.

Ross was delighted with the Planning Commission's report, and with the part he had played in it. The proposed Northwest federal power agency, he believed, was a giant step toward the eventual and inevitable public-power takeover of all electrical distribution systems in the region. Once these systems were in public hands, Ross felt that it was only a matter of time before the private utilities of the area were seen for the inefficient, outmoded firms that he had deemed them to be. The Power Trust, J.D. Ross predicted in 1937, is doomed in the Northwest.

On July 16, 1938, Samual Insull died in a Paris subway of a heart attack. Although exonerated by the courts, in the eyes of the public Insull had been, in the last years of his life, a representation of all that was wrong with the old ways of conducting a business. He had become a symbol of all the false hopes, the pipe dreams, the inflated expectations of the thousands who had put their trust in the slips of paper that had come out of his pyramid. What seemed saddest at his death was a general acknowledgment that Insull really hadn't meant to cause suffering to anyone, that he himself had become trapped in the paper pyramid he had built by the same illusions of power he had inspired in the hearts and minds of the hapless investors.

# 2

# PUBLIC POWER CONSOLIDATES
# IN WASHINGTON STATE

Ken Billington likes to tell people that he was married twice in 1938; first to his wife, and then to the Crusade for Public Power in Washington state. The anecdote took on a new meaning for him when he arrived at the office of the Washington Public Utilities Districts' Association in 1951 as its new executive director. There, he was to find a "dead horse" case's legal bill of $2,200, the salary of the one secretary due, only $300 in the treasury, and squabbling among the public utility districts that made up the Association. One of the first phone calls Billington received in his new office was from a PUD manager who called to say that another manager had been of the opinion that there were too many public power organizations and that therefore he planned to recommend to his PUD's commission that they drop out of the Washington PUD Association. Billington's response to his caller was short, "Do me a favor. Call that other manager back and tell him the sooner he gets out of the Association, the sooner I'll know how many districts I'll be serving." Ten minutes later, the other manager called Billington to say that he hadn't really meant what he had said about getting his PUD to quit the Association and that he had only meant to suggest ways to improve the group. Again, Billington's answer was to the point: "I don't have time to go around selling the Association to its own members and still do the work needed just to keep it alive. If you want out, go ahead. Just don't waste my time."

For better or worse, Billington was in this public power crusade for life.

The PUD laws passed in Washington and Oregon in 1930 gave a new definition to the crusade in the Pacific Northwest. In previous years, the power wars had been carried on from strongholds in Seattle and Tacoma, with isolated public-power fortresses in towns such as Eugene, Oregon; Centralia, Washington; and Bonners Ferry, Idaho offering what little support they could. The plans for battle, the objectives, the cause's course were all very general during those years. In fact, simply being against private enterprise's monopolization of electric power put one in league with the Northwest public-power movement—whether one advocated federal ownership, state ownership, municipal ownership, PUD ownership, or a combination of these—and regardless of whether one might have opposed the legitimacy of none, some, or all of the rights of any institution to any or all of the generation, distribution, or marketing facilities of the electric industry. Up to 1930, no particular path for developing new power sources manifested superiority or even favorability. But on November 4 of that year, the state PUD laws received the mandate of the Oregon and Washington constituencies, and the PUD then became clearly the way to go, at least in Washington.

The case was not so clear in Oregon, where the PUD law was more restrictive, and this was to mark a significant parting of the ways for energy development in the two states. In Oregon, only four people's utility districts were formed after 1930, although after the completion of Bonneville Dam a dozen small, publicly owned cooperatives were organized to bring the project's power to remote rural areas. The vast majority of the state's population occupied the Willamette Valley from Eugene to Vanport just north of Portland, territory securely held by two Portland-based power companies. Thus, public power was never to make a considerable impact in Oregon.

In Washington, on the other hand, public utility districts were easily established, typically using county boundaries to define their service areas. By 1936, the number of these county PUDs in the state was 34. Most of these were not yet "activated," that is, they were not providing electricity; they were anticipating the purchase of cheap power from Grand Coulee Dam in 1940. In the meantime, some PUDs were buying surplus power from municipals. A few took over little farm mutual companies; Mason County PUD No. 1 became the first activated district in 1935 in this manner. In order to fund these ventures, and to build their transmission systems, the PUDs relied heavily on issues of revenue bonds. Just prior to the completion of Grand Coulee, private interests attempted to throw a roadblock in front of the PUDs' plans to purchase the dam's electricity by sponsoring Initiative 139, a state bill that would have severely hampered the districts' ability to issue revenue bonds. With its defeat, the way was wide open for the PUDs to borrow freely for the purpose of financing their power projects.

Throughout the 1940s, the PUDs acquired electric properties and facilities mainly through two methods. The first method used a legal maneuver mastered by a young lawyer affiliated with the PUDs, Jack Cluck, to file condemnation suits against private utilities. The suits challenged the right of investor-owned utilities (by this time known in all sectors by the abbreviation IOUs) to acreage which the IOUs had bought ostensibly for the purpose of siting a power plant or putting up transmission lines. This was called the right of eminent domain. According to state law, if the land-owning utility did not develop its land for power purposes within a certain period, the right of eminent domain would pass to any utility with the means of so developing that land.

The second method the PUDs employed to acquire property and equipment was through negotiated sales. Their main man in these cases was a fiscal agent with impeccable Wall Street credentials: Guy Myers. It was through Myers that J.D. Ross had been able to obtain vital financing for the Diablo Dam project on the Skagit in 1933. Ross had first appealed to Interior Secretary Harold Ickes for funding from the Public Works Administration for the dam, which Seattle City Light would build for the benefit of western Washington PUDs and municipals. But Ickes had refused, pointing out that the state of Washington had already used up its appropriations for Grand Coulee. Ross had tried other federal avenues to no avail before finally turning to Myers, who then introduced Ross to eastern financiers. Ironically, the public power magnate had been turned down by an administration favoring public power and, in the midst of the Depression, had been befriended by the allies of his mortal enemies in the Power Trust: the New York bankers. Ross had had a great admiration for Myers, who assisted in financing public power project throughout the United States. Myers recommended to the Washington PUDs, as he did to Ross, that they rely heavily on the sale of revenue bonds, as opposed to general lien bonds.

Myers' endorsement of revenue bonds was based on a principle that was to become the keystone for the PUDs' fiscal policy for the next fifty years, ending in catastrophe in 1983: *Public utility revenue bonds are payable only from income from future power sales.* This is in contrast to municipal bonds, which become the general obligation of the municipality, to be repaid primarily by municipal taxes. The state is obliged to place limits on a community's debt from the sale of general lien bonds, in order that tax burdens do not become excessive. Such limits do not apply to revenue bonds because the bonds cannot be retired by using taxes to pay the principal. And, the yields of revenue bonds issued by PUDs are not subject to federal income tax, as are revenue bonds sold by federal agencies such as the Tennessee Valley Authority. Thus they are considered tax-free, an attractive feature to the bondholder. The beauty of these bonds, from a PUD perspective, is that they are both agency-specific and project-specific; that is, the county PUD has sole responsibility for retiring the debt on the revenue bonds. Other county agencies or county-sponsored projects would be unaffected.

As the PUDs of Washington shared the financial consulting services of Myers in planning their economic futures, it became apparent to them that they were all drawing on a pool of expertise formed by professionals who were friends of public power: Cluck served as the PUD legal advisor, and Robert W. Beck, an engineer with Seattle City Light, was their engineering consultant. The Washington State Grange had been acting as coordinating agency for all inter-district activities and meetings, and was instrumental in bringing an awareness of the mutual and interrelated needs and objectives of the state's PUDs. On December 7, 1936, Fred Chamberlain, who was state Grangemaster, called a meeting of all 34 Washington PUD commissioners at Grange headquarters in Seattle. There, with the help of Chamberlain, Cluck, and Beck, the Washington PUD Commissioners' Association was organized. Later, because PUDs began to be run by managers instead of commissioners (not to mention the fact that the group's title was already too long), the name was shortened to the Washington PUD Association. Its purpose was to act on matters of mutual interest and benefit to its members, to represent its members before state and congressional committees, and to compile and distribute information on its member districts to all interested parties. Such a role would not seem to predestine the PUDs for greatness; the founders of the Association were pragmatists, after all, whose expectations for the future went no further than a hope in strength through unity. As it turned out, the districts needed more than mere unity to acheive a dominant position in regional affairs—they needed vision, innovation, perseverance, and a touch of diplomacy. They got it in Ken Billington.

Billington came out of a logging camp near Stephenson, Washington, in 1938 as a young man with interests that lay far beyond the tall stands of timber that were the livelihood of his lumberman father. Billington certainly did not fit the woodsman stereotype: short, bespectacled, unobtrusive, he was not to become a recognized leader of the stature of J.D. Ross. Yet his influence in charting the course of public power in Washington was to be enormous.

For Billington, it began in the home of state Democratic Chairman Elwood Caples in Vancouver, Washington. Billington had come to Vancouver from Stephenson to work as a personnel clerk for the Federal Works Project Administration. Caples had been instrumental in getting the young man the job, so he invited him to his home in order that they get better acquainted. The other dinner guest that evening was none other than Senator Bone, running for reelection. Bone was in town to help the local Democrats drum up support for an initiative to establish a PUD in Vancouver's Clark County. In the course of his conversation, the senator challenged Billington to join the public power crusade. Billington knew little about the deeper undercurrents of the struggle, but was so impressed by Bone's zeal that he stayed up until 3 a.m. listening to Bone explain his reasons for carrying on the fight. Later that same morning, the lumberman's son went out and volunteered his services to the Grange leaders who were working to get the Clark County PUD initiative on the ballot. Billington had enlisted for his first sortie of the crusade; what he didn't know is that he would be in it for the next 43 years.

At first, Billington was just another PUD activist, spending most of his spare time working through the Grange to assist in the activation of Washington PUDs. There was a wholesomeness and integrity in the crusade and its followers that was intensely appealing to Billington. It was, as he was to call it later, "power development, grass-roots style." Its objective was as American as apple pie: to seize the mysterious powers of electricity from the grasp of technocrats shielded by the Power Trust in order to put those powers under the direct control of the average man and woman. The fact that the odds against the advocates of public power were so great made the crusade that much more exciting. Even with all the legitimacy of the New Deal mandate behind them, the crusaders were underdogs, pressing against the monolith of the private utilities with every meager resource they could muster. There was no question that to be part of such a cause meant sacrifice. PUDs in the 1930s operated on a shoestring and a prayer; their allies in the Grange held potlucks and bake sales to raise money for paying legal bills or buying advertising or hiring engineers. Everyone knew that the power companies could match every dime of that money with a dollar, and often they did, particularly before an initiative vote or election, when the private interests would shell out huge sums of money in trying to defeat a referendum or candidate representing public power. But Billington knew that what the crusade lacked in its treasury it more than made up for in people. Time and again, he witnessed the faith that the great majority of the people of Washington state put in consumer-owned electricity. And why not? The simple, accessible structure of the public utility district was undeniably democratic in its style. The most basic PUD consisted of a commissioner to handle the business end (finances, contracts, customer relations, etc.) and an operating manager to take care of engineering concerns. As the PUDs grew, the commissioner became a board of commissioners, and the manager was given responsibility over an engineering team divided into specialized functionary roles of power operations. But the commissioner or board of commissioners of any district remained directly accountable to the consumer-owners of the county who paid the rates. The commissioners were elected representatives; if the PUD's customers didn't like the service, or if they thought the rates were getting too high, they could replace their commissioner in the next election or by recall. And, according to the state PUD law, the commissioner was required to hold a job in the community from which he earned a living *outside* of his elected role. In other words, the commissioner was forbidden to ever become a professional PUD bureaucrat; he was obliged to remain a layperson whose only distinction in the community involved the extra duties of directing the county utility. Of course, this was not the case with the PUD manager, who was hired instead of elected, and whose business—in those formative years of PUD development—was simply to keep the "juice" flowing. Later, as the operations side of some PUDs became increasingly important, managers took the leadership position from commissioners, which tended to fuzz lines of authority and responsibility. It was the first in a series of steps that would eventually lead to disaster.

An event in 1944 was to change Billington's status to a leadership position in the PUD movement. At that time, he was personnel director for Kaiser Engineering's shipyards at Vancouver, doing his part in cranking out Liberty ships by the dozen to fuel the war effort. Word came to him through the Grange that the Washington chapter of the populist Public Ownership League had become active in the cause of PUD property acquisition, and was sponsoring a candidate for the state legislature on the Socialist party ticket out of the Washington

PUD Commissioners' Association's offices in Seattle. This upset Billington and some of his Grange compatriots, who were concerned that the Association, which they were wholeheartedly supporting, would become identified with a fringe group whose philosophy was anathema to all but the most left-leaning in the mainstream public power movement. So, they organized a "Public Power League," with Billington as president, for the express purpose of offsetting the Public Ownership League's presence and influence in PUD matters. Not long after that, Billington helped to move the Association offices to a new location a few blocks away in order to assure that the break with the supporters of socialism was complete.

After the war, Kaiser wanted to move Billington to its automobile plant in Ann Arbor, Michigan, but his roots were too solidly embedded in Northwestern soil and in the crusade for him to leave Washington. He was deeply embroiled in assisting opposition to an anti-PUD initiative that the private interests had succeeded in putting on the 1946 electoral ballot. Eventually he quit Kaiser and in 1948 became personnel director of Clark County PUD in Vancouver, which had just acquired the local properties of Puget Sound Power & Light. It was the same PUD which Billington had helped to establish when he first entered the crusade a decade before.

Billington remained president of the Public Power League, which served primarily as a political planning and organizing center for the region's publicly owned utilities. He attended all of the state PUD Association's meetings in Seattle, where he became well acquainted with the Northwest's movers and shakers of public power. Public power was well represented at the beginning of the 1950s. Beside the League and the PUD Association was another organization called the Northwest Public Power Association (NWPPA), which, along with the League, was headquartered in Vancouver. The NWPPA served a function similar to that of the PUD association, but its scope of interest was wider, encompassing all publicly owned utilities in the entire Pacific Northwest, including British Columbia and Alaska. Its director was Gus Norwood, who often acted as a spokesman for public power to the federal agencies in Washington, D.C. NWPPA's office was on the Columbia River just across from Portland; on the side of the building facing the Oregon city and spelled in 10-foot-high red neon were the words PUBLIC POWER—a reminder to ratepayers in the private-power domain on the Oregon side of the river of the reason why their Vancouver neighbors were paying three times less for their electricity.

In 1951, Billington was asked to fill the position of executive director of the Washington PUD Association. When he assumed his post, the Association was in a state of near crisis. Disputes had split the ranks of the group's members between public utilities that had acquired their properties and wanted the Association to coordinate their operations, and PUDs that were still trying to obtain property and were afraid of getting left behind by the power-oriented members. Other districts felt the Association should be abolished altogether. In addition, a regionwide shortage of hydroelectricity threatened to make the feuding irrelevant by debilitating all PUD power systems equally. And hanging all over this was a growing tension in the nation's capital between remnant New Dealers and the waxing forces of quasi-militant conservatism, which looked unfavorably on the rise of PUD influence in the state of Washington. Billington saw the political storm clouds gathering on the horizon and knew that 1952, a presidential election year, was going to be pivotal for the continuing crusade.

The Bonneville Power Administration (BPA) marked its fifteenth year of existence in 1952. From its rather modest beginning in 1937 as a local agency to market wholesale power from Bonneville and Grand Coulee dams, it had soon become the linchpin of the regional power network. As more dams had gradually been added to the federally owned Columbia River Basin Power System, BPA's responsibility and power domain had grown. Congress, which maintained strict control over BPA's purse strings, had added to the agency's duties by broadening and defining Bonneville's service area and services. By 1952, the agency was marketing 61 percent of the entire power supply of an area embracing 200,000 square miles—two-thirds of the vast Columbia Basin.

BPA was never intended to be modeled after its older and bigger Southern sister, the Tennessee Valley Authority; the Northwest's public-power heritage would surely have made a TVA-style system an alien presence. For another thing, TVA was given authority to construct and operate its own power-generating facilities, often financing them by means of revenue bond sales. Bonneville, on the other hand, was given the burden of the debt from the region's federal dams, which were built and operated by the Army Corps of Engineers with funds taken directly from the U.S. Treasury. To this day, BPA is repaying the Treasury with the revenues collected from BPA's sales of power to its customers: investor-owned utilities, PUDs, and others. Therefore, BPA has always been less autonomous than TVA in its relationship to Congress. This fact did not figure much into regional matters until

1947, when ideological changes in Washington, D.C., had a profound impact on Congress's perception of BPA's role in the Northwest.

J. D. Ross had been the natural choice for the position of BPA's first administrator. He accomplished a great deal in his two years as BPA's founder-chief, but his masterwork was the regional transmission grid, which distributed hydro-generated electricity from Grand Coulee in central Washington to the California border, northern Nevada, and the foothills of the Rockies in western Montana.

Ross's legacy was in shaping Bonneville's character into one that was so fundamentally regional that, when Paul J. Raver took over the agency's Portland headquarters at J. D.'s death in 1939, it didn't matter that Raver was not a native Northwesterner. What did matter (aside from the fact that he was a good friend of fellow Chicagoan Harold Ickes) was that he had been a public utility economics professor at Northwestern University for many years, and that he had served as chairman of the Illinois Commerce Commission during its investigation of Samuel Insull's utility empire in 1934.

These credentials ensured that Ross's successor would carry on the publicly oriented spirit embodied in the Bonneville Project Act which had legislated BPA into existence in 1937. The most monumental of four major policy declarations in the act was one that contained what became known as the "preference clause": "...the administrator shall at all times, in disposing of electric energy generated at said project, give preference and priority to public bodies and cooperatives."

To the Northwest's publicly owned utilities, this short phrase was a benediction, affording them a decisive advantage over the IOUs. As a general rule, he who controlled the region's hydropower resources controlled its energy policy, and he who had the controller's first favor wielded the greatest influence over the direction of that policy. That controller of energy policy has, since 1937, been the Bonneville Power Administrator, and the publicly owned utilities (the "preference customers" in BPA nomenclature or, simply "publics") enjoyed by right the biggest pull on BPA. Later, the growing complexity of the region's energy situation and the entrance of new interest groups on the scene would crowd the publics' influence. But, in 1940, public power was in its best form ever. Activation of PUDs was under way across the state of Washington, Administrator Raver was a benign Big Brother, and the IOUs were in retreat following the failure of Initiative 139.

However, America's entrance into World War II would mark the beginning of a gradual erosion of the public's preeminence. In 1942, in keeping with the War Department's philosophy that the war would be won in the air, the newly organized War Production Board ordered Seattle's Boeing Company to manufacture 75,000 warplanes a year. For its task, Boeing would require mammoth supplies of aluminum; so, the board directed the Aluminum Company of America to build massive plants near Bonneville and Grand Coulee in order to have direct access to the dams' power. Aluminum production, a highly energy-intensive industry, extracted such a large bloc of electricity from BPA that the Alcoa plants became among BPA's biggest customers practically overnight. The increasing demands for war-related industrial output spurred the board to order BPA to coordinate an agreement among all the region's utilities, both public and private, to cooperate in order to meet wartime electrical loads. Thus was born the Northwest Power Pool (NWPP), a joint operating and planning pact of the Northwest's utilities, built around the exchange and sale of bulk power transmitted via BPA's grid.

The Power Pool had a purely technical function, but its establishment nonetheless had economic and political ramifications that did not end with the war. By 1945, sales of federal power to the IOUs had grown so large that they could not be abruptly halted. And higher-than-normal riverflows on the Columbia, along with additional power-houses installed at the federal dams to meet wartime demands, had led to a surplus of available federal power in 1945. Power left over after public utilities had used as much as they could was sold to the IOUs.

Another actor that had entered the BPA limelight with the IOUs was the aluminum industry. It had been a virtual charge of BPA during the war; therefore, when the demand for aluminum slackened at war's end, Raver felt compelled to assist the private companies which had resumed ownership of the plants from the government. Many economists feared a postwar recession, and Raver wanted to do all he could to head off the widespread unemployment that would result from a shutdown of the aluminum plants. At Raver's urging, the government stockpiled aluminum ingots to prop up lagging sales. But instead of stagnating, the U.S. economy soared, and aluminum sales soared with it. The aluminum companies had thus become a permanent fixture in BPA's policy-making process. They came to be known as direct-service industries, or DSIs, because they buy their power directly from BPA, whereas the region's other industries purchase electricity through a public or private utility. With the IOUs and DSIs vying for BPA's attention, the influence of the preference customers was undermined almost as soon as it had begun.

The end of hostilities overseas signaled the resumption of the power war in the Northwest. Roosevelt's death and the resurgence of Big Business foretold the private utilities that the aggressive public power policies initiated by the New Deal were soon to wane. However, in October 1949, Raver urged Congress to appropriate funds for construction of two more federal dams, in anticipation of what BPA forecast as unprecedented electric load growth. The IOUs realized that any new federal dams in the region would merely increase the amount of power to which the publics would have first rights. Therefore, in January of 1946 four Northwest power companies—Washington Water Power, Pacific Power & Light, Northwest Energy Company, and Puget Sound Power & Light—issued a joint memo which stated that *they* predicted large power surpluses in the near future.

Largely on the basis of that memo, Congress decided to postpone further discussion of the dam appropriations until after the elections that fall. Raver had been embarrasingly upstaged. However, rather than opting for confrontation with the IOUs, Raver invited them as well as the publicly owned utilities to a conference in Tacoma for the purpose of talking over the differences in load forecasts. About the only thing everyone agreed on at the end of the meeting was a need for more inter-utility communication on perceived future energy demands.

The IOUs' success in stalling the federal dams gave them the confidence to have another try at blocking PUD expansion, which was continuing apace in Washington. Thus, Initiative 166 was placed on state ballots in 1946 and given a rousing campaign by private interests. Like Initiative 139 in 1940, I-166 sought to restrict the ability of PUDs to issue revenue bonds; again, the attempt to choke the flow of funds to the publics went down to defeat at the polls.

But the preference customers' "Big Brother" in Portland was not so fortunate. On the same day that I-166 lost in Washington, Republicans won enough seats in Congress to regain the control they had lost in 1932. The following year, the House Appropriations Committee drastically slashed BPA's budget request for that fiscal year. The committee report deplored the Washington PUDs' "un-American practice" of condemning private utility property, and strongly recommended that BPA stay out of such affairs. The events of 1948 were even more ominous. A Columbia River flood which obliterated the Portland suburb of Vanport was paradoxically followed six months later by unusually low water conditions, resulting in debilitating shortages of power up and down the entire West Coast. The four private utilities that had predicted surpluses in the scurrilous memo of 1946 were subjected to sharp criticism from three states. Subsequent studies showed that the shortages could have been avoided by power exchanges over a Pacific Northwest-California linkup. Raver went before the Appropriations Committee in the spring of 1949 to plea for Congressional approval of the linkup. Despite the support given Raver by most of the Northwest's congressional delegation, the Bonneville administrator was again rebuked by the committee. Citing the continuing condemnation proceedings by the Washington PUDs, Committee Chairman Ben Jensen of Iowa charged that BPA was conducting a public-power vendetta against free enterprise. Additional appropriations were refused. Following this second setback, Raver had no choice but to curtail BPA activism on behalf of public power.

The House committee's parsimony had power planners in the Northwest wondering where future hydroelectric supplies would come from to meet the region's rapidly growing loads. The answer came shortly after the United States entered the Korean War in June 1950. A Defense Power Administration (DEPA) was formed in the Interior Department for coordinating power needs as the country once again was put on a war footing. DEPA granted numerous "certificates of convenience and necessity" for waterpower projects deemed to be "defense oriented"; these certificates allowed companies to write off up to 56 percent of project costs against corporate income taxes in five years. Thus, the IOUs had the unprecedented economic incentive they had been wanting in order to make dam building a profitable enterprise. Power shortages in the Northwest in 1951 and 1952 encouraged the companies to expedite construction on the region's rivers. Anxious for a solution to the recurring brownouts, Northwesterners turned their hopes for new power from the financially crippled BPA to the booming private sector.

On July 9, 1952, Ken Billington called a meeting of a handful of key PUD managers and commissioners at the office of the City Light superintendent in Seattle. Also present were the superintendent of Tacoma Light and Gus Norwood from NWPPA. Billington had called them together to discuss the future course of PUD affairs in light of the challenges brought on by the contingencies of the time.

The public power leaders were all well aware that the PUDs were passing into a new era. The establishment of new districts had peaked in 1936 and had run its course by 1940. Acquisition of private distribution systems by the publics had occurred mainly between 1939 and 1949; the purchase of Snohomish County's electrical system by its PUD in 1949 had marked the final activation of all county PUDs in the state. With BPA withdrawing from new power generation, at least for the foreseeable future, it was clear that the next step for the PUDs was to build their own generating systems. Indeed, Pend Oreille County PUD, in the extreme northeast corner of the state, was just beginning construction of a modest dam. But in order to compete with the private companies, who were aggressively pursuing major hydro projects, the PUDs would have to undertake some big projects themselves. Some PUDs adjacent to the Columbia were already making initial studies of undeveloped sites on the river. But it would take more than initiative to dam the mighty Columbia; it would take massive financing of a type that even the region's major IOUs might have difficulty raising. There were reports that the IOUs were discussing among themselves the possibility of forming consortiums consisting of two or more companies, which would share the costs and benefits of cooperative efforts in dam construction.

Billington put forward the rhetorical question: Why can't public power have the same economic benefits of joint corporate planning and construction as private power? Even with the accelerated amortization offered to the IOUs by DEPA, publics could still build and operate power plants cheaper than could the private companies, mostly because of the financial advantages of public utility revenue bonds over corporate debt financing. Why couldn't several PUDs get together on a project and issue enough bonds as a group to take care of all the funding needs?

Billington was aware that such an effort was already being pursued by two PUDs seeking to purchase some of Puget Sound Power & Light's generating facilities; the Association had secured a law in 1949 which permitted PUDs a "partnership association" on joint projects. But ownership and bond issuance had to be made in the name of each participating district. What the PUDs really needed, stated Billington, was a "joint operating agency": an institutional framework backed by state law which would actually consist of a number of PUDs but which nevertheless would be considered a single entity for financing purposes. As a single entity, the joint operating agency (JOA) would combine the credit powers of member utilities for the purpose of constructing and operating power projects.

The meeting's attendees discussed specific concerns with respect to the proposed JOA, then a committee was formed to draft a measure for introduction to the state legislature. The committee—Harvey Davis, an attorney for Chelan County PUD; Dean Barline, a Tacoma Light lawyer; and Billington—drafted the proposed JOA law. A major concern in the formulation of the law had to do with authority and responsibility in the relationship between the PUDs and their joint operating agency. The JOA, as defined by the draft law, was to be no more than an appendage of the public agencies, the "construction and operating arm of the member utilities," and as such it would have no policy-making powers except in a purely technical capacity. In other words, the board of directors of the proposed agency would act as a representative body of the member utilities in making decisions on their mutual objectives, and the JOA's manager-engineers would then carry out those decisions. What may or may not have been known by those who understood the JOA law was that it effectively removed by one more step the access that the consumers (the ratepayers) had to the electricity they owned.

With the legislation for a JOA law drafted, the bill was ready for introduction to the legislature in Olympia. But first it would have to get past Governor Arthur B. Langlie.

Langlie was not a friend of public power, which would seem extraordinary for the top official of PUD-infested Washington, conservative Republican though he was. However, neither was he, in 1953 at least, clearly a foe of the publics, nor an ally of the private companies. Yet his seemingly neutral position, particularly his refusal to support Washington's congressional delegation in pleading for federal resource-development appropriations, caused irritation among advocates of public power. When Langlie read the draft JOA law, he informed PUD representatives that he wanted to reintroduce a 1949 law which was to have established a Washington State Power Commission (SPC), empowered with many of the same functions as the proposed joint operating agency. Langlie proposed that the Power Commission law be amended to include provision for a public joint operating agency, to be approved by the Commission. The PUDs had to accept the compromise. They recognized that the legislature would not approve Langlie's Commission without the support of the local utilities; conversely, without the governor's approval, the JOA law could not be enacted. However, before they accepted the amended Commission bill, both private and public utilities insisted that the new law contain a prohibition against the Power Commission ever usurping a hydroelectric site by filing a competing application after a utility had already filed.

The agreed-upon State Power Commission law was passed and the governor activated the Commission. The PUDs and municipals met and decided that the proposed JOA would construct Priest Rapids

Dam on the Columbia River as its first project. The dam site had already been researched by Grant County PUD, which had also filed an application with the Federal Power Commission to construct on the site.

On January 22, 1954, an application for the formation of Joint Operating Agency No. 1 of the State Power Commission was submitted to the Commission by representatives of 14 PUDs and seven municipals. The application was tabled on March 26, despite strong protests from the single PUD representative on the five-member Commission. No action one way or the other ever was taken on the application.

In July, Congress extended authorization for construction of Priest Rapids for a limited period of time to Grant PUD or other agencies. Time was running out on Grant County's preliminary permit; construction would have to start soon or the county would forfeit its claim to the site.

The Power Commission's next move was unexpected, to say the least. Instead of approving the joint operating agency, the SPC filed a competing application with the FPC for Grant County's dam site. Grant PUD, however, secured a court order restraining the SPC from any further activities relative to Priest Rapids until the legal right of the Commission to engage in such activities had been tested in court. With the SPC tied up in litigation, the PUD was able to pursue another plan for funding the dam, and went ahead with its plans for construction. . .without the JOA.

Some public power people accused Langlie of betrayal, but Billington was not interested in speculating on the governor's intentions; all Billington wanted was a joint operating agency free of constraints by the Power Commission, and he was willing to put the screws to the SPC to get it. On February 18, 1955, the Washington Supreme Court denied the SPC a right to file against Grant County for Priest Rapids. With the legitimacy of the court decision buoying them, Billington and state Senator Nat Washington (who was also Grant PUD's attorney) went to Olympia and rallied their supporters in the state House of Representatives to put a block on any appropriations for the SPC. It wasn't long before the two men were called from the legislative arena to the governor's office.

They arrived to find Langlie visibly upset. He demanded to know why Billington and the PUDs wouldn't agree to using the SPC for their power supply purposes. Billington told him that it was very simple: The organization that controls the power supply of a utility could also control the utility. The choice thus was between control by a politically appointed commission or control by the locally elected officials governing the local public power utilities. It was the opinion of those utilities, stated Billington, that decisions, good or bad, which obligated the revenues of a local utility's ratepayers should be made by the locally elected utility officials.

Langlie shot back: "Then why do you rely on the federal government for electricity?"

Because no specific interest could get dominating control of a federal agency, Billington replied, and the preference clause was a policy supported by both political parties no matter who is in office. He then delivered an ultimatum: Either the PUDs got control over the organization that was going to be their power supplier, or they would depend on the federal government and the preference clause to keep private power-influenced politics one step removed from what rightfully belonged to the publics. More specifically: "Either we get an amendment to the law that will remove our joint agency from control by the State Power Commission or not one penny of appropriations will be forthcoming."

The square-off eventually ended in a victory for the PUDs. Langlie conceded an amendment to the law which had established the Power Commission, removing from SPC authority the right of JOA approval. Billington was careful not to make the mistake he had made in drafting the first joint agency law; in the new law, the power of JOA approval was transferred to the director of the State Department of Conservation, and a clear procedure was provided whereby "arbitrary or capricious action" by that individual could be challenged in the courts. In fact, approval was made automatic unless there was a legitimate challenge. Billington was certain that many legal and political hurdles lay ahead, and he was determined to forearm the legitimization process for a future joint agency.

With the JOA formation mechanism in place, the PUDs returned to their own separate, autonomous concerns. Several districts followed Grant and Pend Oreille counties' lead and began plans for building dams on their own, without the joint operation appendage. The arrangements that they had to make in order to construct the dams were not entirely satisfactory to the PUDs, but it was not until more than a year had passed that they again decided to press ahead with organizing a JOA. More rumblings from Washington, D.C., cued Billington to introduce a resolution at the June 29, 1956, meeting of the board of directors of the Washington PUD Association. The resolution called for all interested PUDs to join in forming a new joint operating agency.

The name of the agency was to be the Washington Public Power Supply System.

# 3

# THE PARTNERSHIP POLICY

The reasons for the formation of the Washington Public Power Supply System (WPPSS) have their roots in the so-called partnership policy of the Eisenhower Administration.

McCarthyism was rampant when President Dwight D. Eisenhower took office in 1953, and the prevailing fear of creeping socialism caused the federal institutions to shrink away from policies and responsibilities that they had inherited from the New Deal. The postwar boom had fostered a general public willingness to return to the laissez-faire attitude which government had more or less been following in its relationship to the private sector before the Depression. This attitude was reflected somewhat in a number of federal programs that sought to place the initiative for control of basic social services in private hands.

Eisenhower unofficially kicked off his partnership policy in his first State of the Union address:

> The best natural resources program for America will not result from exclusive dependence on Federal bureaucracy. It will involve a partnership of the states and local communities, private citizens and the Federal Government, all working together. This combined effort will advance the development of the great river valleys of our nation and the power that they generate.

These words seemed to be aimed directly at the long-lived confrontation between public and private power in the Pacific Northwest. The substitution of partnership for confrontation marked a fundamental shift in the institutional relations governing the development of the regional power supply system. For in the reference to "private citizens" Eisenhower encouraged full participation by the investor-owned utilities in power planning, as well as in the power ownership. This was actually the culmination of a trend that began with the formation of the Northwest Power Pool in 1942. The trend gained momentum in 1950, when the Defense Electric Production Act made investment in the new power facilities a highly attractive option for the IOUs. At the same time, the federal "Big Brother" of the public utilities was under attack. The Edison Electric Institute (which had succeeded the infamous National Electric Light Association during the 1930s, inheriting most of its patrons and interests in the process) characterized the Bonneville Power Administration as "socialistic" and representative of federal "encroachment" on the private utilities. The *Reader's Digest* branded BPA Administrator Paul Raver a "socialist." Fortunately, those observations from outside the region were not generally held in the Northwest. BPA and the publics had some very vocal supporters in the U.S. congressional delegations from Washington, Oregon, and Montana, and they were often able to modify and deflect through legislative action the administrative policies that began in the executive branch.

But the Northwestern representatives in Congress could not break the chokehold that the Interior Department had put on federal dam-building projects in the early 1950s. One by one, the dozen or so dams planned by the Army Corps of Engineers and Bureau of Reclamation around the region were crossed off the list of federal appropriations. The "partnership policy" became known by its detractors as the "no new starts" policy. When private power interests began to pick up the project sites and plans that the government had dropped, Democratic advocates of public power sarcastically redubbed it the "giveaway policy." Nowhere was the giveaway policy more dramatically challenged than in Hells Canyon. This 25-mile reach of the Snake River at the bottom of the United States' deepest gorge, which divides Oregon and Idaho, was to be the focus of a monumental war between public and private power that would draw the interest of the nation.

The opening shot of the war was fired in 1947, when the Idaho Power Company (IPCO) applied to the Federal Power Commission for a preliminary permit on a minor dam at Oxbow in Hells Canyon. The Interior Department promptly protested, stating that it was contemplating a high dam and large storage reservoir further up the canyon as part of BPA's Columbia River Basis System. Interior was

wary of IPCO; the Boise-based private utility had carved its own private-power domain out of most of Idaho except for the panhandle and
scattered rural areas. IPCO had been exempted from the NWPP in
1942 since it did not serve any defense-related industries, and when
the NWPP was granted permanency at war's end, the Idaho company
declined to join.

Thus, IPCO was seen as a bit of a maverick even by other IOUs in
the region, which were all participating in coordination of planning
and development in the NWPP. When IPCO changed its application
from one dam to a string of five, four other power companies began
discussing how they might act jointly to prevent a complete takeover
of the Middle Snake River by IPCO.

By 1952 IPCO had modified its five-dam plan to one having three
low-head dams, and the Department of Interior had intervened in
favor of the government's single High Dam project. Meanwhile, the
issue had attracted public power leaders and conservationists, who
formed groups in Idaho and Oregon to press for "comprehensive,
multi-purpose development" of the canyon. Naturally, the federal
High Dam plan met most of their criteria.

Enter the Eisenhower Administration. On May 5, 1953, the administration put its "partnership policy" to its first real test by directing the Federal Power Commission to withdraw Interior's petition of
intervention in the Hells Canyon case. Immediately, the leaders of
the Hells Canyon interest groups reacted to the crisis by forming the
National Hells Canyon Association (NHCA), an amalgam of labor organizations, rural electric cooperatives, farmers' organizations, citizens' groups, and concerned individuals. The group representation was
estimated by the Association as over two million people nationwide.
Once again, the Oregon and Washington Grange organizations were
instrumental in cultivating grass-roots support. But the core of NHCA's
leadership were two Washington PUD managers: Vincent Cleveland
from Clark County, and Owen Hurd from Benton County. Ken Billington from the Washington PUD Association and Gus Norwood from
the Northwest Public Power Association often acted as officers in
the NHCA.

As a result of the NHCA effort before the FPC, the scope of the
Hells Canyon hearings broadened to include flood control and navi-
gation benefits as issues, along with the obvious concern of low-cost
power—all of which, argued the NHCA, favored a federal High Dam.
But the NHCA lost all three skirmishes in this particular battle: It lost
before the FPC with the Commission's issuance of a license to IPCO

on July 27, 1955; it lost in the federal courts, where it had tried to appeal the FPC licensing; and it lost in Congress, which failed to authorize legislation for the federal dam. Billington lobbied intensively in Washington, D.C., for legislative action on behalf of the NHCA, but he expressed frustration due to "biased and false statements made by private power representatives which have been lent credence by the 'parrotting' of Governor Langlie. . . ." In spite of support by the majority of the Northwest's congressional delegation, the first battle in the Hells Canyon fight went to Idaho Power.

On September 7, a whole new front was added to the war when the Pacific Northwest Power Company (PNPC) applied to the FPC for a license to build Pleasant Valley Dam about 20 miles downstream from the IPCO dams. PNPC was a joint operating agency that had been formed by five Northwest-based IOUs: Pacific Power & Light, Portland General Electric, Montana Power, Washington Water Power, and Mountain States Power. (Interestingly, the companies had been watching the Washington PUDs' frustrated efforts at forming a JOA under the Washington State Power Commission in 1953; they then decided to incorporate PNPC on April 13, 1954, in Salem, under more amiable Oregon legal conditions.) NHCA filed as an intervenor in the Pleasant Valley hearings in its continuing advocation of a federal project.

The entrance of another private entity into the Hells Canyon fray caused consternation in some members of the Washington PUD Association. They reasoned that if private enterprise succeeded in locking up the Middle Snake, the government would then feel justified in abandoning other areas of the region where it used to have grand designs, on the premise of breaking up what one Interior official of the time called a "Federal monopoly of the power business by BPA and other government agencies."

But by the mid-1950s several PUDs resigned themselves to the "partnership policy" as a fact of life. These were the districts that straddled the last undeveloped stretch of the American reaches of the Columbia, which runs mostly south to bisect the center of Washington state from just below Chief Joseph Dam to the mouth of the Snake near Pasco. The PUDs wanted their own dams there, but they could not raise the necessary funds on their own. When Grant County PUD nearly lost Priest Rapids Dam because of the delays associated with the Washington PUD Association's failed attempt at forming a joint operating agency, its manager sought the avenue many in public power had vowed they would never take: "partnership" with the IOUs. J. D.

Ross himself had predicted in 1936 that such a compromise was against the principles of public power:

> Any attempt at a partnership, it is safe to say, has never been a success, and never can be a success. You cannot make a partnership between a concern that carries its indebtedness forever when its structures have rotted into the earth, and whose ideal is to make dividends on that perpetual capital cost, and a concern that rapidly pays out its debt, and whose ideals are for service instead of profit. Any compromise of a rate between these two would be injurious to the public when their proper right is a lower rate.

However, Grant County felt that it had no choice; if it didn't agree to partnership, it couldn't build the dam. If it didn't build the dam soon, it would lose its license on the dam site; an IOU or private joint agency would probably then build its own project on the site for the exclusive use of private utilities. Thus, Priest Rapids became the first joint venture between investor-owned and consumer-owned utilities. After half a century of often bitter competition over power development, the two sides finally agreed to a shared arrangement on a project. Other PUDs followed Grant County's example, eventually bringing to five the number of hydropower projects built under partnership agreements, all on the main stem of the Middle Columbia. The PUDs initiated all of them; even so, they had to grit their teeth when they signed the contracts. For although the publics would own and operate the dams with funds financed through its revenue bond sales, the projects would be paid for with capital from the IOUs, which of course then insisted on the lion's share of the resulting power. It was a precedent-setting arrangement: public financing provided the economic advantages of tax-exempt, low-interest operation and maintenance, while the private sector provided the capital.

The public-private construction projects of the mid-1950s might have seemed to mark a truce in the Northwest power wars, or a fundamental concession on the part of the publics. Not so. Events in 1955 had reduced the enthusiasm for public power, but they had not *turned it back*. The dramatic reversals in the next year would demonstrate that the crusade was at its best when circumstances looked worst.

Like 1952, 1956 marked both an election year and a turning point in the fortunes of the Washington PUDs. Once again, portentious events in the nation's capital sparked a consolidated response by the public utilities. A Senate investigation revealed the most sordid affair involving private power since the Federal Trade Commission hearings on NELA 25 years before. The administration's efforts to cripple the Tennessee Valley Authority by negotiating a deal with the Dixon-Yates private utility syndicate embroiled it in a costly fiasco. It was discovered that Eisenhower actually wanted to sell the TVA, but he had overplayed his hand, and the government wound up in the embarrassing position of having to sue to cancel as "contrary to public policy" the contract it had negotiated. The news that the administration had been trying to sell TVA struck a sensitive chord in the Washington PUD Association. It was seen as a direct threat to BPA as a federal entity, and that meant that the privileged status of preference customers such as the PUDs was also threatened. Billington called together the board of directors of the association on June 29 in Seattle, where they drew up a resolution aiming to form their previously sought joint operating agency. The resolution called on all PUDs to join in the formation of the JOA, to be called the Washington Public Power Supply System, by August 1. The JOA law required that the agency be advertised in the county or counties in which it planned to construct or operate facilities. The directors agreed that Billington would advertise WPPSS in each of all 39 counties of the Association so that, as he put it, "if Eisenhower carried forth his threat to sell BPA, the Association would have a public power agency in Washington to buy out every line and substation."

There was a strong possibility that an attempt to bring WPPSS into existence would spur litigation to block it, but the PUDs were not daunted. They reasoned that a suit against their consolidated plans would have the benefit of adjudicating the entire JOA law—provided the case ended with the PUDs on top, of course. Grover Greimes, director of Clallam County PUD, was nominated and eventually elected as the first chairperson of WPPSS. Coincidentally, the first legal challenge to the embryonic joint operating agency came from Greime's county.

On August 1, with 16 county PUDs signed on as WPPSS participants, the anticipated lawsuit was filed in Clallam County against the county PUD by R. L. Keeting of Dungeness. Keeting alleged that the state law under which the PUDs sought to form WPPSS was unconstitutional because 1) the title of the law was not a clear description of the JOA act, 2) there was no provision for hearings at which ratepayers could complain against any proposed venture of WPPSS, and 3) PUD commissioners did not have the authority to advance county funds for joining such a project. The constitutionality of the law was upheld in Clallam County on September 7. Shortly thereafter the state

Supreme Court concurred, giving the PUDs the adjudication for WPPSS that they had sought.

On October 8, 1956, 17 PUDs (Okanogan County had joined after August 1) filed an application for approval of WPPSS with W. A. Galbraith, director of conservation in Olympia. Under the JOA law, Galbraith was to advertise the intent of the PUDs for four weeks, after which he had 90 days to approve. Galbraith was an appointee of Governor Langlie, whose sentiments regarding PUD joint agencies were well known, and there was speculation that the governor might attempt to block the JOA through Galbraith, once the four-week advertising period was over. But on November 6 Langlie was resoundingly defeated in the elections, and then the question was whether Galbraith might not approve WPPSS out of spite for his former boss's trouncing. These reckonings were made irrelevant when the new governor replaced Galbraith as director of conservation with Earl Coe, a public-power sympathizer.

The ousting of Langlie was only part of a general political turnover in the Northwest from the 1956 elections that was shattering in its thoroughness, destroying any chance that the government could pawn off BPA. In every key race, the voters expressed their profound dissatisfaction with the partnership policy. The causes of this malaise can be traced primarily to two factors: the 1956-57 recession, which made voters eager for new policies; and a regionally ingrained distrust of the power companies. The bitter feelings of the Dixon-Yates scandal lingered after the matter was resolved, leaving private power shaken. Public power groups smarting from their setbacks in 1955 saw a chance to assume the offensive. Nowhere was the attack more forthright than on the issue of Hells Canyon.

At the beginning of 1956, the Hells Canyon situation was a struggle for political as well as geographical turf. The NHCA had filed in the U.S. Court of Appeals opposing the FPC decision authorizing IPCO's three low dams on the Middle Snake. With the help of the Washington PUD Association, the NHCA continued to lobby Congress for a bill to construct a federal High Hells Canyon Dam near PNPC's Pleasant Valley dam site. The argument in Congress over federal involvement in the development of the canyon became increasingly strident. The issue had become an ideological touchstone by which loyalty to the president was measured. Leading the fight for the Senate bill for a federal dam were the Democratic delegations from Washington (Warren G. Magnuson and Henry Jackson) and Oregon (Wayne Morse and Richard Neuberger). They often sparred with Senator

Herman Welker of Idaho, who championed IPCO's projects. Magnuson and Morse were up for reelection, so the Republicans chose two out and out "partnership" enthusiasts to run against them. Opposing Morse was Douglas McKay, who had quit his post as Secretary of the Interior in April in order to make a bid for Morse's seat. It was McKay who had ordered an end to his predecessor Ickes's intervention in IPCO's site filing, which had set off the Hells Canyon fight in the first place. McKay had also ordered BPA to sign 20-year power sales contracts with IOUs as a first step toward the privatization of the federal agency. Running against Magnuson for the Senate was none other than Governor Arthur B. Langlie.

The NHCA was running candidates out of its own ranks against the administration's supporters. Most of them had little or no political experience, but they enjoyed massive financial campaign contributions from the NHCA's nationwide, grass-roots network. They were up against the full force of the administration, which by midyear viewed Hells Canyon as the crucial test of its entire domestic policy. In July, the Senate bill for a federal dam in Hells Canyon was defeated 51-41. One Republican senator said he had received six phone calls on the issue from the White House and the Interior Department in the days before the vote, asserting, "The pressure, in the opinion of many senators, is as great as that applied on any issue in the last three years."

But if the conservatives thought that their victory in July was a foretaste of the elections that November, they were severely mistaken. On the morning after Election Day, the Republicans would wake up to a political carnage in the Northwest. The Democrats swept the races in Oregon and Washington, and won a few important posts in Idaho and Montana as well. Magnuson won more handily than anyone. Langlie was more or less forced out of office; he had run for Magnuson's seat partly because he didn't stand a chance at being reelected to the governorship. His landslide defeat effectively ended his political career. In the other Senate races, McKay lost to Morse, and Welker was soundly beaten by a long-time leader of the Boise chapter of the NHCA, Frank Church. In the House, the most vocal opponents of federal hydropower development, Harrison Ellsworth of southern Oregon and Sam Coon from the eastern part of the state bordering Hells Canyon, were defeated. Coon was eased out of the contested area's back yard by a young real estate agent named Al Ullman.

There is little doubt that public power groups played a crucial role in the extraordinary Democratic resurgence. Working with meager budgets similar to those of the 1930s, the crusade showed a strength that the White House had badly underestimated. Perhaps the only public-power loss in the region during that election was one in Stevens County surrounding Spokane. There, voters decided to sell the county PUD to a private utility, the only such transaction in the state's history. A few days later, at a conference of utility leaders in Tacoma, Billington was talking to Paul McKee, president of Pacific Power & Light, about the Stevens County vote. The PUD executive wished aloud that the PUDs had as much money as the IOUs to spend on political causes such as the one in Stevens County, where the companies had spent a great deal to convince voters to sell their PUD. McKee replied, "Ken, for the votes you publics have in this state, we'll trade you our dollars any time you want them."

Eisenhower easily retained the presidency in 1956, but his partnership policy was solidly repudiated. McKay's resignation as Interior Secretary in his failed bid for the Senate turned out to be another big mistake for the administration, which bowed to congressional pressure to fill the post with a more progressive policy maker. On June 9, publisher Fred Seaton from public-power-dominated Nebraska became the new head of Interior, where he provided a climate that eventually promoted BPA back to its position of benign Big Brother to Northwest publics.

On the Snake River, however, the fight between public and private interests were far from over. The U.S. Supreme Court had okayed, with provisions, Idaho Power's right to build its three low dams in Hells Canyon. The NHCA and its public power allies finally conceded that battle to IPCO, and turned their full attention northward to the lower canyon, where Pacific Northwest Power had filed for the Pleasant Valley project. On January 20, 1958, the FPC denied a license for Pleasant Valley. The NHCA did not have long to savor the victory, because two months later PNPC filed for a site ten miles downstream from Pleasant Valley, where it proposed to build a larger dam called High Mountain Sheep. The project envisioned a reservoir that would back water over 20 miles upstream, to the tailrace of IPCO's northernmost dam. But the NHCA received its greatest disappointment on June 2, when the last congressional bill for a federal Hells Canyon Dam was killed by the House Interior Committee. Throughout 1958 1959, the NHCA used various tactics to delay the FPC hearings on High Mountain Sheep for as long as possible. Owen Hurd, the public power leader who also served on NHCA's executive board, hinted broadly that the Washington PUDs were putting together a Hells Canyon proposal of their own as a consumer-oriented replacement to the dead federal dam project, but that they needed more time.

Finally, the FPC would be delayed no longer. On February 1, 1960, the Commission ordered that hearings on High Mountain Sheep commence March 21. On March 15, a public-power agency based in Kennewick, Washington, filed with the FPC for a hydropower project on the Middle Snake that was huge enough to rival PNPC's dam. For most people, even those of the Northwest, it was the first time they had ever heard of the agency. The name of the newly proposed project was Nez Perce.

The name of the agency was the Washington Public Power Supply System.

# 4

# WPPSS: THE FIRST YEARS

The Washington Public Power Supply System was born in the office of the state director of conservation, Earl Coe, on January 31, 1957, seven months after its conception in Seattle the previous June. It was a humble event. The stroke of Coe's pen that approved and thus created the Supply System was not accorded even the anonymity of a back-page paragraph in any newspaper. Nevertheless, the handful of commissioners and managers from the 17 member utilities of WPPSS who were able to be in town to witness the signing of the order recognized the historic significance of the event: it was the culmination of four and a half years of legislative and legal battles. For Lars Nelson and Jack Cluck, who were also on hand, the birth of WPPSS was the fruition of efforts which, for them, began over 20 years before at the founding of the Washington PUD Association.

The first meeting of the WPPSS board of directors was convened on the morning of February 20, in the Seattle offices of the PUD Association. Aside from the 17 board members present were Cluck, Robert W. Beck (who by that time had his own engineering firm, which was at work on several of the PUD-IOU "partnership" dams), and of course Ken Billington. The meeting had to be moved to the Admiralty Room of the neighboring Roosevelt Hotel to secure more space. There, the founding fathers of the Supply System adopted its first three resolutions: 1) to undertake preliminary studies of construction of possible power projects, 2) to open a WPPSS bank account, and 3) to obtain a $100,000 surety bond as the initial operating budget of WPPSS.

By its fourth meeting, in May, the WPPSS board had elected a five-member executive committee, which was to meet at least once a month. Two other early decisions were the selections of Beck's company (R. W. Beck & Associates) at the initial WPPSS engineering consultant, and Cluck's firm (Houghton, Cluck, Coughlin & Henry) as WPPSS legal counsel. The PUDs making up WPPSS brought at least a dozen project proposals to the meetings for discussion. Most of them involved small hydropower projects.

Meanwhile, some quick thinking in Olympia was to give WPPSS an unexpected advantage for the future. There, the state legislature was undertaking a housecleaning of policies and programs left over from the Langlie Administration. The 1956 state elections had turned control of the governor's office and the state senate to the Democrats, and a Democratic house had been retained. Therefore, without any coaching on the part of the PUDs, the state legislature abolished what it saw as an ineffectual holdover of the partnership policy: the State Power Commission.

As usual, Ken Billington was in the right place at the right time. As the legislature dismantled the Commission, he was watching the proceedings from the gallery when an idea struck him. Motioning his friend Nat Washington off the Senate floor, Billington hurried down, took the state senator aside and said, "Let's put in an amendment saying that all the powers heretofore granted the State Power Commission will be transferred to any joint operating agency that wants them." Washington did, the amendment passed, and the broad legal, fiduciary, and operating powers of Langlie's junked Power Commission were immediately inherited by the Supply System.

The next order of business was to hire a managing director for WPPSS. There was a strong move by some member utilities to hire Frank Ward. Ward had been superintendent of Tacoma Light when he attended the 1952 meeting that conceived the JOA law, then had become the managing director of the State Power Commission when it was launched by Langlie in 1954. With the Commission abolished, Ward was looking for a job. But there was bad blood between Ward and some WPPSS members, because Ward had instigated the SPC's 1955 over-filing of Grant County PUD's Priest Rapids site.

The logical choice then was Owen Hurd, who had had a long and solid commitment to public power, which had involved him on county, regional, and national levels of leadership in various representative organizations. He had been manager of southeastern Washington's Benton County PUD for ten years, and had just moved the PUD's offices from the county seat of Prosser to the town of Kennewick when he was invited to become the first WPPSS managing director. He accepted, and left his Benton PUD post for the Supply System, which provided him a $16,000 yearly salary, a step up from the $13,000 he had been earning at Benton.

On November 15, WPPSS approved establishment of WPPSS headquarters in Kennewick, for the simple reason that it was where Hurd lived. At the time, Kennewick was a commercial hub for the area's cattle ranchers and sheep herders, as well as a residential community for the government-employed Hanford workers. Hurd had built himself a house in Kennewick before his call from WPPSS—that was why he had transferred Benton PUD's offices there—and naturally he was in no mood to move again. The other WPPSS members were noncommittal about a headquarters locale; at that point the Supply System didn't even have a permanent secretary, so it didn't really matter where it had its phone answered. Meetings of the executive committee continued to be held at the Stewart Hotel in Seattle, readily accessible from the 17 member districts scattered across the state. Hurd settled into his office in Kennewick, and from that day the fates of WPPSS and the Tri-Cities were irrevocably locked together by events that were even then focusing the attention of the U.S. Congress on a piece of government property only a few miles north of the new WPPSS office—the Hanford Atomic Works.

Hanford played an integral part in ushering in the atomic age 15 years before. In 1942, the top-secret Manhattan Project was launched by the Allied powers in their race to beat Germany to effective development of an atomic bomb. The project scientists realized that they needed large amounts of the artificial element plutonium in order to build the bomb. And they would need an isolated location, for safety and security, as a site where the plutonium-producing reactors could be constructed. The Army and the project's designer, the DuPont Company, found the ideal place at Hanford, a tiny community of about 100 on the dry, gently rolling rangelands of southeastern Washington. Just east of town, the Columbia cut a wide blue swath through the grey sagebrush, bringing ample cold water, a necessity for cooling the reactor during the fission process. Just west of town, a Bonneville Power line brought electricity from Grand Coulee, and thus the large electricity requirement for the project was met. The government bought 600 square miles of uninhabited land north of Hanford and placed the area under the strict cordon of a military reservation.

By mid-1944 Hanford had a peak construction force of 42,400, and the nearby town of Richland had become the biggest boomtown the state had ever seen, covering the barren landscape with drab Army-style dormitories and family units. Only a comparative few of these people knew the true purpose of the facilities they were helping to build on the desert floor, even after they had completed the reactors and shipped some of their plutonium to Los Alamos, New Mexico, in February, 1945. It was not until the following August, after Hiroshima and Nagasaki had been reduced to smoldering ruins, that the people of Richland realized the crucial part they had played in unleashing the awesomely destructive force of the atom.

In 1946, peacetime brought the Atomic Energy Commission (AEC) to Richland. The AEC had been established by the government to continue the production of plutonium for weapons and to promote research in atomic energy. The AEC hoped to accomplish both at the Hanford Reservation. Hanford no longer existed as a town; it had been replaced by a complex of reactor buildings, laboratories, and research offices—a collective still known simply as "Hanford." It was operated under a contract with the government by General Electric, which had purchased it from DuPont. GE was interested in the feasibility of using waste heat from a plutonium-producing reactor to generate electricity. In 1953, GE took its proposal for this "dual-purpose" reactor to Congress in hope of obtaining federal funding. The 1946 legislative act that created the AEC also established a Joint Committee on Atomic Energy (JCAE), an 18-member panel of members of Congress from both the House and Senate. As a group, the JCAE did not respond favorably to GE's proposal. In accordance with the Eisenhower Administration's philosophy, the JCAE feld that private interests should take the initiative in developing new technologies, without heavy reliance on the government. At least one of the Committee members did not share this view: Senator Henry Jackson from Washington.

Scoop Jackson was blessed with the sort of rare political instincts that made it possible for a Democrat like him to embrace classic Republican themes, act as spokesman for Democratic causes, remain on good terms with both parties, and get reelected year after year. Jackson believed that government subsidies to certain industries had their place—indeed, he would encourage subsidizing of Boeing several times during his career in Congress—and he thought that the infant atomic industry was such a special case. But his colleagues in Congress were wary of government programs that smacked of free-market tampering. They naively assumed that private enterprise would jump into atomic power with all the might of Yankee ingenuity at its disposal, an ingenuity grounded in the unsullied motives of capitalism.

The truth is, in its early years the private nuclear industry built only demonstration plants which were indirectly subsidized by the AEC in the form of rapid tax amortization benefits. Construction of the first commercial atomic power plant in the U.S. did not begin until the Duquesne Light & Power Company, which was to build the plant at Shippingport near Pittsburgh, elicited an agreement in 1955 that saddled the government with all but a minor part of the project's total costs. Encouraged by this precedent, the Consolidated Edison Company applied to the AEC for a permit to construct an atomic power plant in Queens, New York, under a similar arrangement. Nevertheless, AEC Chairman Lewis Strauss came under criticism from the scientific community for moving too cautiously toward commercialization of atomic energy. The scientists pointed out that Britain was already well along on construction of its first commercial atomic power project, and the Soviets were said to be only a short distance behind.

In the Northwest, enthusiasm generated by the promise of atomic energy stemmed from a realization on the part of regional power planners that the hydroelectric potential of the Columbia and its tributaries would be reaching its limit in a few years, when utilities would have to turn to other energy sources to meet rapidly rising loads. Electric loads were growing at the rate of 7.5 percent per year throughout most of the 1950s. Shortly after its formation in April 1954, the Pacific Northwest Power Company (PNPC) negotiated a contract with the AEC for security clearances for selected PNPC engineers, who would be allowed to research the feasibility of a nuclear power plant in the Northwest. A year later, in the midst of partnership policy pressures, two PUDs and two municipals joined with an IOU to form the Puget Sound Utilities Council. This study group had essentially the same purpose as the PNPC work group.

But in spite of all the enthusiastic talk about the imminence of civilian access to atomic power, optimism on the economic feasibility of its production was fading rapidly in the mid-1950s. Both private and public utilities found it difficult to obtain necessary information from the security-conscious AEC. Research costs alone were high. Private companies complained that preliminary research indicated that development and construction of an atomic power plant would result in a prohibitively expensive average of 15-20 mills per kilowatt-hour (a mill is equivalent to one-tenth of one cent). In comparison, the national average production cost for conventionally produced electricity in 1955 was 4 mills per kilowatt-hour.

Two events on the international front awakened the administration to the full implications of its detachment from nonmilitary uses of atomic energy. The first took place on October 17, 1956, when Queen Elizabeth of England pushed a button that resulted in the first release of power into a commercial grid from the Calder Hill nuclear power plant, thus making it the first in the world to begin commercial operation. Critics assailed the AEC for allowing the U.S. atomic effort to lag, but Strauss was nonplussed. He said that the U.S. program was making good progress and that "we have resisted pressures—mainly political—to establish goals of installed kilowatts for a set date. . . ." Instead of building more plants, he said, the United States should be improving the technology. But a former member of the AEC, Henery deWolf Smyth, charged Strauss with using a smoke screen. The real reason that the domestic atomic program was stalled, said Smyth, was due to the AEC's insistence on private rather than public-power development. Smyth had left the commission because of the chairman's superciliousness toward the other commissioners, which seemed to stem from Strauss's privileged status as the president's personal advisor on atomic energy. Using national security considerations as an excuse, Strauss often kept the other AEC members in the dark.

The second international incident came a year after the first, and was even more jarring because it was largely unexpected and, more importantly, it originated in the Soviet Union. On October 4, 1957, the USSR launched its Sputnik satellite into outer space, and the whole issue of U.S. technological competence came to the forefront of national debate; and this time it touched the deepest stirrings of both pride and fear within the American consciousness. The Cold War, said the opinion shapers of the media, would not be won in international marketplaces nor in munitions factories, but in the laboratories. The new weapon in this war was the test tube, and the raw war material was brains—to put Americans into space, to make American technology the most sophisticated on earth. The nation turned to science-oriented committees in government, among other sources, for leadership and direction. One of these, the JCAE, almost immediately seized on a proposal that Henry Jackson had been pushing for nearly a year. It was originally brought to him by the chairman of the board of General Electric. In December, the JCAE recommended the construction of a dual-purpose reactor at Hanford. One member of the committee, Senator John Pastore of Rhode Island, said, "We can't afford to be outdistanced in this atomic program by any other nation." Congress promptly appropriated $3 million to the AEC for the design, development, and engineering work on the project proposal.

Owen Hurd was probably somewhat aware of the new attention being directed at Hanford, but his own interest lay a stone's throw away from the reactor complex, on the reach of the Columbia River just adjacent to the Hanford reservation. The Hanford reach was the last undeveloped section of the U.S. portion of the river, so it was natural that the site would be at the top of the WPPSS list of project options. Ben Franklin Dam was an ambitious plan: it envisioned a concrete-and-earth embankment two miles long, with a generating capacity of 585 MW, compared to Bonneville Dam's 518 MW. Owen Hurd and Glenn Walkley, Franklin County PUD commissioner and WPPSS vice-chairman, had first conceived the dam as a cooperative effort of the Benton and Franklin districts, hence the project's patriotic name. The only major obstacle to Ben Franklin was a tentative disapproval from the AEC, which was concerned about the dam's possible effects on the river waters used to cool its reactors at Hanford. But the technical problems associated with Ben Franklin were minor compared to a series of occurrences that threatened to make the second year of WPPSS its last.

On February 21, 1958, Snohomish County PUD withdrew from WPPSS. Tom Quast, Snohomish's manager, had been unhappy ever since Owen Hurd was selected over Frank Ward as the Supply System's managing director. Quast had served as a commissioner on the State Power Commission while Ward had been SPC head, and was one of the few PUD leaders who had remained on good terms with Ward. There was also the matter of Snohomish's allocation to the WPPSS budget. The size of the allotment from each district was to be based on the district's number of customers, and since it was the most populous PUD, Snohomish was expected to contribute more financially than the other members. The Snohomish commissioners concluded that membership in an unseasoned joint agency wasn't worth the cost.

Whatever the reasons for the Snohomish withdrawal, it was followed in June by Okanagan PUD quitting WPPSS. On August 15, Skamania and Grays Harbor dropped out. The manager of Grays Harbor County PUD was a former navy captain named J. J. Stein, who was known in the PUD Association as an efficient, penny-pinching type who kept a sharp pencil when it came to budgets. There is a good chance that money had something to do with the departure of Stein's PUD; a month before, the AEC had estimated that the cost to WPPSS for providing protection for the Hanford Works from the effects of Ben Franklin would be $15-$25 million. The remaining 13 members of WPPSS realized that their fledgling Supply System was in danger of dying unless it got into some constructive business. WPPSS had existed for over a year entirely on paper; it had no material assets to speak of, only roll after roll of project blueprints. The WPPSS board's worry was not so much that the system might break up as it was that state lawmakers might have regrets about the legislature's part in helping to bring into being a useless joint operating agency and vote to abolish the JOA law altogether. As Billington put it: "We better get pregnant or they'll dissolve us."

So, Hurd informed the next meeting of the executive committee that they were going to decide right there which one of the dozen or so projects under consideration had the best chance of getting quick approval from the Federal Power Commission. Ben Franklin had been dealt a severe setback by the AEC announcement, so it was bumped from the top of the priorities list. The obvious choice, then, was the Packwood Lake hydro project; it was in a remote area (about 20 miles southeast of Mt. Rainier), far from potential intervenors; it was relatively small (27.5 MW); it was economically feasible (around $13.5 million); and it had a simple, straightforward objective. But one of the committee members interjected that, from an economical standpoint, Packwood was a "dog"; its power would be more expensive than BPA's. How am I going to sell the Supply System to my customers, he said, if they have to pay more for WPPSS power? Hurd's reply was that if they didn't build something soon, they wouldn't have a Supply System to sell, because the legislature would do away with it.

The committee elected to go with Packwood. A month later, the project had a preliminary permit from the FPC. The establishment of a clear objective by WPPSS may have helped to stop the defections; only one more district, Pacific County PUD, quit after the Packwood decision. Its January 1959 withdrawal was offset by Wahkiakum County joining the following May, maintaining the number of members at 13.

While WPPSS was committing itself to the Packwood hydro project, Congress was authorizing the construction of a "convertible type" plutonium reactor facility at Hanford. Unlike the existing eight Hanford reactors, the new production reactor (NPR) would not transfer waste heat from the cooling process into the Columbia River; instead, the new reactor would have features that would make it possible to produce plutonium and high-pressure steam simultaneously, the steam being a by-product of the reactor's waste-heat cooling function. The idea was to use this steam to generate a more useful by-product, electric power. The authorization was a hard-won victory for Jackson and other advocates of a direct government push of atomic power. However, the bill did not include appropriation for the facilities that would convert the steam to electricity. The decision to invest in steam-generating equipment for the NPR was postponed to an uncertain later date.

The first firm connection of WPPSS with the NPR project came in January 1959, when the Supply System was invited to participate in a review of AEC reports which were the basis for a congressional decision to back the NPR. The invitation came from a firm which served as the load-forecasting arm of the region's utilities, called the Pacific Northwest Utilities Conference Committee (PNUCC). PNUCC had been formed under the same executive act that established the Defense Electric Production Administration in 1950. A section of the act required that forecasts be made periodically on loads and resources from all parts of the country for ten years in the future. The Northwest Power Pool had been making short-term forecasts since 1942 and some long-range forecasts after the Tacoma Conferences were begun by BPA administrator Paul Raver in 1946. PNUCC was established after these patterns. By 1959, PNUCC was composed of several committees, each having a specific function related to load forecasting and made up of representatives from BPA, the IOUs, the direct-service industries, and preference customers such as PUDs. Like the NWPP, PNUCC was a cooperative effort by all utilities and electric customers in the region: NWPP coordinated actual loads, PNUCC forecasted loads. WPPSS, though not an official member of PNUCC (since it relied on its member utilities for decisions based on their own load estimates), was encouraged to participate in the planning activities of the consortium.

The directors of WPPSS were genuinely interested in taking part in the PNUCC review of the NPR for at least three reasons: First, Eisenhower's partnership policy was all but dead in 1959. None of the regional hydro projects that had been promoted as "partnership" dams had actually turned out that way; the ones that were actually being constructed were federally funded and would be federally owned. And Interior Secretary Seaton was restoring BPA to a dominant role as a regional power broker. Vice-President Richard Nixon, certainly no mean authority on political inroading, blamed the partnership for the 1956 decimation of Republicans in the West, and advised the administration to soft-pedal the policy. Second, WPPSS members had been considering the possibilities of nuclear power even before the joint agency had been formed. Finally, WPPSS recognized that any power project at Hanford (deep in PUD territory) would inevitably have to account for public power's role in some aspect of the project. With these facts in mind, the Supply System's directors formulated a proposal for joint public-private operation of the NPR. Having sent their proposal to the JCAE in mid-1959, the WPPSS turned its attention to the most impressive project on their menu of construction options: the Nez Perce Dam.

Nez Perce represented the last hope for a public-power role in Hells Canyon after the federal government bowed out in June 1958. The FPC could approve only one major project for the Middle Snake reach; there simply wasn't enough room for two large water storage reservoirs in the rather narrow gorge. Therefore, any hydropower proposal that challenged Pacific Northwest Power's High Mountain Sheep Dam would have to carry a clear advantage. WPPSS decided to fill the role that the government had been holding tenuously, as the alternative to private control of the Middle Snake. While the NHCA stalled the FPC hearings on High Mountain Sheep, WPPSS engineer-consultants at R. W. Beck worked out a design for a massive dam that they believed could be built at a cost comparable to that of the PNPC dam, but with a planned generating capacity of 1,200 MW, far surpassing the 875-MW design capacity of High Mountain Sheep. The plan called for the 700-foot dam to be built a few miles north of the Mountain Sheep site, just below the Snake's confluence with the Salmon River. The project was named Nez Perce after a local Indian tribe.

WPPSS filed for Nez Perce on March 15, 1960. A month later, PNPC filed an amendment to its FPC license application, in which the company spelled out its intention to eventually expand its project in a second phase. By adding several more turbines and a larger storage capacity to its planned reservoir, PNPC promised that High Mountain Sheep would have a total capacity of 1,750 MW by 1965, at an estimated total cost of just over $300 million. Those numbers must have looked impressive to the appropriate state commissions in Oregon and Idaho, because in the following few weeks they gave their blessings to the High Mountain Sheep project. That left the FPC license as PNPC's last hurdle.

PNPC's ambitious response to the Supply System's bid forced WPPSS to ask for a delay in the Nez Perce hearings, which the FPC granted. WPPSS engineers went back to the drawing boards to prepare for another round of anteing up. Indeed, what was beginning to look like a high-stakes poker game had implications beyond the Middle Snake, with much more at stake than the 20 or so miles of river in contention. The real issue at Hells Canyon-Mountain Sheep-Nez Perce was the ability of consumer-owned agencies to expand the scope of their activities beyond their traditional responsibilities.

A related concern was that a victory for private power would give Eisenhower and his men cause to resurrect their plans for selling BPA, beginning with the distribution grid skirting Idaho Power's little empire stretching east from Hells Canyon. As Alex Radin, head of the American Public Power Association, warned in December of 1960:

> If the Pacific Northwest Power Company should be licensed to build Mountain Sheep, the consequences would be disastrous. The construction of Mountain Sheep by PNPC would place this powerful combine of utilities in a strategic position insofar as the Bonneville transmission system is concerned and would lead ultimately to the wrecking of the effectiveness of the Bonneville program.

One by one, public utilities around the Northwest lined up in support of the WPPSS proposal, until more than 40 PUDs, municipals, and cooperatives were sponsoring the Nez Perce project. The FPC consolidated the proceedings on the competing Snake River projects, and the fight became even more interesting, pitting the PUDs of WPPSS in direct confrontation with their old private-power enemies. Once again, the crusade had resumed its place at the center of the arena in the main event of the power fight.

With the growing weight of public power's credibility on their shoulders, the engineers at R. W. Beck worked overtime on a dam design on which neither PNPC nor anyone else could possibly improve. At last, the new plan for Nez Perce was finished and with the FPC as an amendment to the original license application. The Nez Perce Dam, as envisioned by WPPSS, was truly awesome: It would ultimately be equipped to generate 3,360 MW, 90 percent more than High Mountain Sheep. In terms of power capacity, it would be the largest hydroelectric project in the world, more productive even than Grand Coulee with its 1,950 MW. The estimated capital cost of $348.5 million would also set a record as the most expensive single power facility ever built; yet that cost meant that Nez Perce power would be the world's cheapest, at a mere 1.03 mills per kilowatt-hour. The battle for dominance on the Middle Snake had caused the contended project plan to grow from 875 MW to a colossal 3,360 MW in the space of only five months.

The show of bravado by the collection of county PUDs behind WPPSS was applauded by public-power advocates across the country. More than a few were incredulous, wondering aloud how the Supply System, with not a single completed project to its name, was going to pull off its mind-boggling venture. But WPPSS had some reason for confidence, for in the month before the submission of its newest Nez Perce plan, the Supply System won a long-awaited prize: a construction license for the 27.5-MW Packwood Lake power project. The licensing marked a crucial step in the WPPSS struggle for legitimacy; as long as it had remained a mere "paper organization" its efforts in the Nez Perce-High Mountain Sheep case would have gone steadily closer to failure. With the construction approval firmly in hand, the Supply System immediately began drawing up the necessary contracts to build Packwood.

The two-fisted plunge by WPPSS into the fight over the Middle Snake, along with the green light on its first project, were proof enough for two former member districts that the joint operating agency was on its way to achieving its objectives. Shortly after WPPSS filed its Nez Perce amendment, the PUDs of Grays Harbor and Snohomish counties rejoined the Supply System and, less than a month later, Cowlitz County PUD became a member for the first time.

The Nez Perce-Mountain Sheep hearings dragged on through early 1961. Then, on April 29, WPPSS dropped a bombshell: It filed an amendment to its Nez Perce license to include a "High Mountain Sheep" plan as a second-choice alternative to Nez Perce. This audacious move stemmed from the WPPSS reading of the Federal Power Act, which specifically requires the FPC to give preference to states and municipalities in issuing licenses. WPPSS filed the amendment in order to clearly place itself in such a preferred position. In other words, WPPSS was declaring that it was ready and willing to undertake the development of the Middle Snake under whatever plan and terms the FPC determined was best, even if it were a project proposed by PNPC. However, the FPC denied the amendment application.

WPPSS made another attempt at gaining the advantage by making its very intriguing project even more attractive. In June it presented design modifications that it said would reduce the estimated cost for Nez Perce from $348.5 million to $308 million. Also included in its revisions was a plan for permitting low-head operation of the project while construction was still in progress, in order to advance the time when power revenues would begin accruing.

These were daring pronouncements, and PNPC made no attempts to match them. The hearings were adjourned in September, and Round One was over in the fight between WPPSS and PNPC, one that would eventually last for seven years.

On the day the FPC adjourned the Snake River hearings, discussions were being held by Coe, Hurd, and Billington which would prove far more momentous for WPPSS. The discussions regarded the feasibility of the Supply System building the electric generating facilities at the Hanford new production reactor.

The conversations came at the end of a legislative battle in Congress that had lasted all summer. The precursor to the battle was a request from the White House in March 1961 for a congressional appropriation of $60 million as an initial outlay of the $95 million needed to convert the NPR to a dual-purpose facility. The new president, John F. Kennedy, had brought into his administration a dynamic attitude with respect to government promotion of new technologies. Kennedy's request was made through an AEC authorization bill, which had the combined backing of the AEC, the FPC, the JCAE, the Secretary of the Interior, and the Bureau of the Budget. But coal and private power interests, led by Republicans Craig Hosmer of California and James Van Zandt of Pennsylvania, attempted to kill the bill in the House before it could go up for a vote. Their position was generally supported by business interests that seized on one engineering firm's study questioning the reactor's capacity to produce steam at a sufficiently high pressure. *Barron's* sarcastically mused that Hanford's low-pressure steam was "more suitable to an old-fashioned locomotive than to a modern turbine." "By way of contrast," editorialized the *Wall Street Journal*, "private utilities across the country are constructing truly advanced power reactors. . . ."

> Free spenders in and out of government have cried against the "shameful waste" of heat energy at the Hanford plutonium plant. . . .The advocates of Government control, once again, have got their wires crossed. Construction of their hearts' desire at Hanford would indeed waste the taxpayer's money and take atomic energy down a reactionary path—an achievement, be it noted, which would be no novelty at all for the dynamos of public power.

The *Journal's* statement that "private utilities across the country" were building commercial power reactors was specious: There were exactly three actually under construction at the time.

In an effort to rescue at least part of the NPR proposal, a compromise was worked out that would cut the federal investment to $58 million for one generating plant. The Senate approved the authorization in September, but the House voted against it a week later.

On September 22, Washington Governor Albert D. Rosellini asked Coe to investigate the feasibility of the state undertaking construction of the NPR generating facilities. Following discussions with AEC and Bonneville officials, Coe believed that the most appropriate entity for non-federal financing of the NPR was WPPSS. Although the Supply System was autonomous of control from Olympia and therefore not a state agency per se, it had nevertheless been organized and empowered by state law. Yet the need for state funding was eliminated by the WPPSS ability to issue revenue bonds, and this fact, from the state's point of view, made the Supply System a logical choice as the NPR's constructor. For the same reason it was a good choice from the federal perspective. And, it was a regionally oriented agency that embodied local initiative and decentralized planning, aspects close to the heart of Republicans in Congress.

When Coe's State Department of Conservation formally asked Hurd and Billington to draw up a proposal for Hanford, the public power leaders were enthusiastic. The request was put before the WPPSS executive committee at an October 20 meeting in Wenatchee in central Washington. The committee instructed managing director Hurd to advise all WPPSS members to come to an early decision on their part in the NPR plan, and to prepare estimates of costs and benefits. On November 28, a formal proposal with basic requirements for NPR electrical generation was submitted by WPPSS to AEC Chair Glenn T. Seaborg.

The WPPSS proposal contained an exchange agreement by which power from Hanford would be integrated with the BPA grid, providing up to 900 MW of electricity to the entire region. According to the proposal, the government would receive between $31 million and $125 million from the sale of steam to WPPSS after power production began in late 1965. During the "dual-purpose phase," when the NPR was producing both plutonium and steam for electricity, the generating costs were estimated to be less than BPA's base wholesale rate of

$17.50 per kilowatt-year. The proposal anticipated that, should the AEC cease plutonium production at Hanford, WPPSS could lease and operate the reactor on its own for electrical generation only, at a cost comparable to that of a coal-fired plant. During this "single-purpose" phase, WPPSS would pay all operating and fuel costs for the reactor and power plant. The proposal enumerated these key benefits of the Hanford project:

(1) To help meet the growing power requirements of the Pacific Northwest, including firming up existing supplies of secondary hydroelectric power for which there is now no market in the region;

(2) To save from going to waste the government's $25,000,000 investment in making the NPR convertible;

(3) To make economic use of steam that otherwise would go to waste;

(4) To improve the fishery resources of the Columbia River system by keeping temperature of the river lower than it would be if the steam were released directly into the water;

(5) To provide peaceful purposes for what heretofore had been mainly military uses of atomic energy; and

(6) To enhance the international prestige of the United States through installation of the largest atomic power facilities in the world.

Legal advisors for the AEC, BPA, and WPPSS all agreed that the contracts for construction of the power plant could be executed without direct congressional approval. Nevertheless, BPA administrator Charles F. Luce was taking no chances on having Congress accuse the Hanford advocates of using the back door to sneak away with government appropriations. On April 16, 1962, he appeared before a House subcommittee to outline the project's details. In his presentation, he stressed that WPPSS was proposing essentially what was a "do it yourself" project for the Northwest, one that would require no federal subsidies, would involve only one extra-regional agency (the AEC), and would actually return money to the federal government. The subcommittee seemed satisfied with Luce's testimony, and WPPSS and its supporters enjoyed momentary relief in the belief that another confrontation with Congress had been skirted. But on July 6, the General Accounting Office (GAO) issued a legal opinion holding that, contrary to the findings of the AEC, BPA, and WPPSS, specific congressional approval would need to be obtained. More important, the GAO ruled that the AEC did not have the authority to sign the contracts that it had been negotiating with WPPSS. The ruling assured another congressional fight over Hanford. WPPSS efforts to avoid conflict had been thwarted.

By the time the JCAE chair, Rep. Chet Holifield of California, convened hearings on July 10, 1962, the battle lines were clearly drawn. Van Zandt of Pennsylvania, representing the coal interests and conservatives in general, led the critics as he had the previous year; Scoop Jackson led the backers. Conspicuous in their absence from the committee hearings were the Northwest private power companies, although they had been specifically invited, and had representatives in town at the time. Public power supporters had been certain all along that they sensed a strong undercurrent of hostility to the Hanford plan despite the fact that the regional IOUs had not expressed their opinions openly. At the close of the first day's hearings, Jackson issued a challenge for the Northwest private utilities to "lay on the line, out in the open" their objections, if any, to the Hanford plan. According to one reporter, the senator was "plainly exasperated by the drone of questions posed by opponents to the WPPSS plan."

The next day at the hearings did not bring a response from the IOUs. However, regional support for the proposal was growing. All 13 congressional representatives from Oregon, Washington, and Idaho urged their colleagues in the House to support the NPR plan. Governor Mark Hatfield of Oregon sent a telegram to Van Zandt emphasizing Oregon's enthusiasm for the energy benefits from Hanford. Rosellini submitted his backing for the record, while Luce and Hurd put in personal appearances before the committee to spell out the virtues of the proposal. The *Congressional Record* grew heavy with testimony in favor of a dual-purpose reactor; yet Jackson was aware that a great deal of opposition lobbying was taking place off the record, behind closed doors, over telephone lines, and in Capitol cloakrooms. He briefly left the hearing room and confessed later that he felt himself "getting weary of this sniping and negative attitude of the private utilities." Then he had an idea. It came right off the top of his head. Without briefing anyone, he hurried back to the hearings to find Ken Billington.

Billington and Hurd were spending a lot of time in Washington, D.C., in those days. They represented WPPSS before the FPC in the Nez Perce-High Mountain Sheep hearings, and before the JCAE in the NPR hearings. Billington was sitting in the audience at the latter proceedings when he noticed Jackson enter the room from behind the committee and take his place at the table. To his surprise, Billington saw Jackson motion to him to come up and join him. He was even more startled when he heard what the senator had to say. The only way to get the project off dead center, Jackson told the PUD leader, would be to compromise and give half of the power output to private power companies in the Northwest. Billington said that this was a bitter pill to swallow after all the private opposition to the plant, but he agreed that it might be the only choice for WPPSS. Then he asked for 24 hours to get approval from each PUD member of the Supply System.

Billington got in touch with Hurd, who shared his reluctance to make a deal with the IOUs. He had, after all, invited the companies to participate in joint operation of the NPR in his 1959 proposal to the JCAE, and their response then, as in 1962, was to try to kill the project entirely. But the two men realized that a compromise was probably the only hope they had. They spent the next two days making phone calls to the WPPSS directors, who agreed to the compromise.

The JCAE endorsed Jackson's amendment giving private utilities 50 percent of NPR's power. On July 17, the House took up the AEC authorization bill. By this time, California's Hosmer had switched to a position of support of the bill, but Van Zandt was still heading the attack. Van Zandt came up with an amendment stipulating that the AEC not be authorized to enter into a contract with WPPSS to build the proposed steam plant. The Van Zandt amendment passed, 232-163, and it appeared that the Hanford project was finally dead.

The Washington PUD Association solemnly gathered on July 20 in Wenatchee to consider the next move. Other public-power supporters were there, including APPA general manager Radin. The atmosphere of gloom was little cheered by editorials from newspapers around the country, which condemned the House's arrogant attitude toward the public interest. The association adopted a resolution urging the Senate to approve the Hanford project and further urging the House to reconsider its vote. Hurd then returned to the nation's capital to offer what support he could to Jackson, who remained undaunted in his determination to get the WPPSS steam plant built. On August 1 he introduced the AEC authorization measure to the Senate, where it was approved.

Again, the issue went to the House, where Van Zandt made a motion to kill the bill in committee. This time, proponents of the project won a round when the House voted against the motion. The WPPSS project was showing signs of gaining ground in the house.

What followed was one of the more extraordinary lobbying efforts in congressional history. Again, the 13 members of the Northwest congressional delegation sent a bipartisan appeal for support of the Hanford project to their fellow members, and a few of them put in extra time and effort in attempting to persuade colleagues to switch sides. The publisher and editor of the Kennewick *Tri-City Herald*, along with Governor Rosellini, flew to Washington, D.C., to lobby on behalf of the NPR steam plant. Letters from Northwest residents backing the proposal came to Capitol Hill in a flood. Hurd and Billington continued as mainstays of the fight. Rep. Hosmer, who had helped lead the opposition to Hanford in 1961, had become one of its staunchest advocates in the summer of 1962, wheedling his fellow Republicans with arguments that focused on the "do it yourself" aspects of the NPR. On September 14, the House voted 186-150 in favor of the Hanford project, and on September 26, Kennedy signed the AEC authorization bill.

Only six and a half years before, WPPSS had consisted of a piece of paper and a dream in the hearts of ordinary men. Against sometimes overwhelming odds, the Supply System had managed not only to survive, but to earn the privilege of ushering the nuclear age into the Northwest. The blessings of the president himself, from the seat of power in his Camelot-on-the Potomoc, were on the WPPSS venture in the desert of that far corner of the United States. Indeed, the eyes of the nation were on the collection of county electric utilities that would complete what would be the world's largest nuclear power facility. The dream that began in the darkest hours of the public power crusade had become a reality at last. But there was another reality that lay 20 years ahead, one that no one could have foreseen in 1963.

There was a nightmare beyond the dream.

# 5

# THE JUGGERNAUT

A year to the day after he signed the Hanford Generating Project's bill into law, John F. Kennedy stood on an outdoor stage splashed with brilliant sunshine. Behind him sat the congressional contingent of the state of Washington, Governor Rosellini, public-power leaders, civic officials from the Tri-Cities, and assorted dignitaries from the AEC, BPA, and other interested agencies. Before him, 37,000 people stood or sat on folding chairs, camp stools or lawn lounges. They were on essentially virgin soil. That day, the government had opened the Hanford military reservation to the public for the first time in observance of these ground-breaking ceremonies for what had become known as the Hanford Generating Plant (HGP). The NPR reactor, which would produce the heat for the HGP's steam supply system, stood, newly completed, a short distance away. The atmosphere was charged with celebrations. Bright helium balloons dotted the crowd, multi-colored beach umbrellas added a holiday touch, and kids and grown-ups wore all manner of hats and improvised headgear to shade themselves from the broiling September sun. The youthful president, his hair glinting with each gentle desert breeze, spoke of the "giant sword" forged at Hanford to end the Second World War. With the same skills used to create that sword, declared Kennedy, "our nation is now forging a plowshare." He then waved a uranium-tipped wand over a radiation counter on the stand, energizing an automated power shovel that, with one scoop of bone-dry earth, began the foundation of a new phase of energy development in the Northwest.

For the Washington Public Power Supply System, the future seemed to shine as brightly as the desert sun that broiled the crowd that day. The crusade reached its zenith in the following decade. Throughout the 1960s, WPPSS occupied an enviable position by the standards of any electric utility. As late as 1970, the Supply System's permanent staff numbered only 66, and it retained the simple, decentralized framework that had inspired so much confidence in its customers. The electric rates of its member utilities remained among the lowest in the world, yet service was always reliable and courteous, the type one would expect from a county PUD. It was almost inconceivable that such an organization could be constructing a facility that would utilize the most complex and mysterious technology on earth. But in June 1964, at the completion of its Packwood Lake hydroelectric plant, WPPSS proved that at least it possessed innovative engineering capabilities. The Supply System pointed with pride at Packwood Lake's "example of how a power plant and nature can coexist in harmony." By keeping most of the project's structures underground, and foregoing any kind of dam construction, the pristine Cascade Mountain setting was largely preserved. It was a long way from Packwood Lake's 27.5-MW plant on the cool, heavily forested slopes of Mt. Rainier, to the 900-MW steam-generating system alongside the nuclear reactor on the tumbleweed-blown flats of Hanford. But WPPSS believed it could span that technological and logistical gap just as surely as forests and deserts could be encompassed within the single state of Washington.

The Hanford Generating Project put WPPSS in the major leagues; in 1963 the Supply System was finally working at a financial scale and level of technical sophistication comparable to those of the IOUs. Unlike the IOUs, WPPSS did not set rates or forecast loads, but otherwise it had the same powers and responsibilities of any other utility. And the ideological gulf that had separated public and private entities seemed to have been bridged by the sharing of the NPR's output. The public-private rift appeared to heal further as the Columbia River hydro system reached maturity with the upper basin development of 1964. (These involved complicated coordination agreements between investor-owned and consumer-owned utilities on both sides of the United States-Canada border.) Even the war between WPPSS and the Pacific Northwest Power Company ended unexpectedly in 1967. It was to prove a Pyrrhic victory for both sides.

The truce on the Middle Snake was preceded by three and a half years of the toughest legal battles in the history of the struggle. On

February 5, 1964, the Federal Power Commission issued a license to PNPC to construct and operate High Mountain Sheep Dam. Two of the FPC's commissioners, David S. Black and commission chair Joseph C. Swidler, dissented on the grounds that WPPSS was the party entitled to the license because it had a preference under the Federal Power Act. By this time, the Department of the Interior had rejoined the fray to argue that the federal government was best qualified to build a dam on the Middle Snake. Interior Secretary Stewart Udall joined WPPSS and the Washington State Department of Conservation in filing with the FPC for reconsideration of its license order to PNPC. Years of legal maneuverings followed, until WPPSS and the Department of the Interior succeeded in taking the case to the U.S. Supreme Court. On June 5, 1967, the Court ruled 6-2 that the FPC should reconsider its order licensing PNPC to build High Mountain Sheep. The case was formally remanded to the FPC for further proceedings consistent with the Supreme Court's opinion "that determination. . .be made only after an exploration of all issues relevant to the 'public interest' including future power demand and supply, alternative sources of power, the public interest in preserving reaches of wild rivers and wilderness areas, the preservation of anadromous fish for commercial and recreational purposes, and the protection of wildlife." The Court did not rule on the WPPSS preference claim.

The FPC, which perhaps had thought back in 1964 that its license issuance to PNPC was the final word in the case, may have been weary of the whole business of Middle Snake development by the time the Supreme Court handed down its decision. Certainly the commission took an unusual step when it ordered all parties in the case to attend a conference in Portland on September 28, 1967, in order to expedite the "orderly conduct and disposition of further hearings." Each party was to make a statement of its position and outline the scope of future presentations of evidence. On the first day of the pre-hearing conference, the two long-time adversaries in the Nez Perce-Mountain Sheep fight made an extraordinary announcement: WPPSS and PNPC had agreed to undertake as a joint venture the development of the High Mountain Sheep reach of the Snake River.

The stated objective of the agreement "is to prevent possible delays in the project's construction and to minimize financial and other risks resulting from the prosecution of competing license applications by the parties." They also invited the Interior Department to "join in whatever extent possible." Interior was so completely taken aback by the utilities' big surprise that it was unable to state any position; two weeks later Udall asked for a delay in the start of hearings for at least four months. The FPC denied the secretary's plea. On January 4, 1968, WPPSS said it would no longer maintain application for the Nez Perce project on the Snake, and would not assert any claim of public preference to a license. In turn, PNPC said it would not assert any claim of priority against WPPSS.

What had happened in 1967 to bring about this seemingly perfect harmony between the two old warrior-entities? One could point to factors that could easily suggest that the parties were getting worn down by what for all practical purposes looked like a stalemate on the Snake River: time (March 1968 would mark eight years since WPPSS first filed for Nez Perce), money (a total of $9 million expended by both applicants by 1970), and energy (by April 1970, 577 witnesses had testified in the course of the proceedings, producing an accumulated total of 28,461 pages of transcript and 1,436 technical exhibits). But according to those who were close to the case, the essential reason for the public-private agreement on High Mountain Sheep Dam was a phenomenon which was later informally but aptly termed in more than one power planning document "the Juggernaut." The Juggernaut was and is simply the political and economic character of the technology of thermal power and all that that character implies. For the heritage of hydroelectric power in the Northwest, it implied a great deal.

The Juggernaut was unleashed on July 11, 1962, when Senator Henry Jackson moved to break the deadlock in the congressional hearings on the Hanford project. However, it would be unfair to blame Jackson for what followed from the Juggernaut's release because it was destined to happen in any case. The Juggernaut had been lying in wait for years before 1962, and every utility person and power planner in the Northwest knew it and dreaded it. Indeed, it was none other than Owen Hurd and Ken Billington who in 1959 first proposed a joint public-private effort in constructing the HGP and sharing its output. Therefore, Jackson's dramatic compromise proposing an alliance of public and private interests was surprising only in its timing; the inevitable fact already known to both sides was that a jointly-owned thermal plant was going to have to come sooner or later. That fact was brought into material terms with the HGP ground-breaking in 1963. However, it would be three years before a regional commitment to thermal development was made. It was natural that Charles F. Luce would initiate the commitment.

Luce was a native Washingtonian who made a name for himself as the attorney for local Indian tribes in their fight for fishing rights on the Columbia River. He identified closely with Northwest aspirations, and his term as Bonneville Power administrator was highlighted by sure, innovative policies and programs which put BPA back into a position of leadership in regional energy matters. In 1966, he examined the region's situation in light of its hydroelectric traditions. For almost 30 years the entire Pacific Northwest had enjoyed the economic advantage of the lowest-cost electricity in the nation due to the hydropower generated at the great federal dams throughout the Columbia Basin and distributed to every corner of the region over the BPA system. By 1966, a total of 22 federal dams were pouring over 6,000 MW into BPA's lines, and eight hydro projects under construction would add another 8,000 MW. But the hydroelectric potential of the region, enormous as it was, was rapidly reaching its limits. Increases in demand for power, on the other hand, were higher than ever. Luce concluded that the utilities of the region had put off building large thermal plants for long enough, and they all knew the reason why: It would require a cooperative effort by the forces of both sides of the power struggle. BPA, Luce decided, was the only actor in the long drama of public-private confrontation with the means to bring about an agreement on joint thermal development.

The thought of sitting down with 110 squabbling utility organizations of varying pedigree, ownership, and economic interest in order to hammer out a peace treaty must have been daunting indeed to administrator Luce. Not until after he had been called to an undersecretary's post at the Interior Department did Luce appoint a special task force to study thermal additions to the regional grid, with the ultimate objective of bringing together the utilities to plan for those additions. Luce left the matter in the hands of David S. Black, who succeeded him at the end of 1966.

Black had been serving on the FPC and had made a name for himself during the Nez Perce-High Mountain Sheep hearings by continually insisting that WPPSS was the proper agency for developing the Middle Snake, a stance that had put him at odds with most of the other commissioners, but had endeared him to the publicly owned utilities of the region. In October 1966, he convened the first meeting of the newly formed Joint Power Planning Council (JPPC) in Portland. In light of the regional utility past, the JPPC represented a level of public-private cooperation that bordered on the radical. Certainly by 1966 there had already been nearly a quarter of a century of joint efforts, beginning with the formation of the Northwest Power Pool in 1942, and continuing through the Tacoma conference in 1946, the founding of the Pacific Northwest Utilities Conference Committee in 1950, the consolidated energy research groups such as the Puget Sound Utilities Council in the mid-1950s, and the Coordination Agreement in 1974 involving public and private agencies in the United States and Canada. However, in each instance, every utility had approached regional needs only on the basis of its own individual objectives. Bonneville always acted as the representative of the Northwest good, distributing regionwide the benefits of utility self-interest. The "partnership" dams of the mid-1950s began an erosion of the traditional autonomy each power agency had enjoyed for so long, primarily because they were the first large non-federal additions to the regionally integrated system. They signaled the start of a larger role taken by the utilities in constructing power facilities on their own. Constructing dams in the hydro-abundant Northwest was one thing; building a thermal plant, however, was a whole new ball game.

It wasn't as if the region's utilities had never built a thermal plant. Some of them had built "steam plants" that ran on fuel oils, diesel oil, or natural gas, but most of them were small, producing a maximum of only 1-2 MW. Large thermal facilities were prohibitively expensive to operate because of high fuel costs; the Northwest, while endowed with water power, is poor in other energy resources. It has no oil to speak of, little natural gas, and only a few deposits of low-quality lignite coal. Most of these fuels would have to be imported into the region to run any non-hydro power facilities, and transportation costs for all of them have always been high. The one thermal-power exception to this rule is nuclear energy, which has comparatively low fuel costs. This fact was the primary factor behind the keen interest in nuclear power expressed by the region's utilities since the dawn of the atomic age.

Capital financing of large thermal plants presented another economic hurdle for the utilities. A basic problem was lack of equity. In all areas of the country, except the Northwest and Nebraska, IOUs dominate, so that capital investment can be easily financed through corporate bonds backed by the assets of privately owned power companies; in the Northwest, where IOUs account for only half the retail sales of electricity, the private assets available to finance expansion were only half as great, proportionally, as those of other regions. Most of the publics were not in a much better position; they owned little property because they had relied on the federal government to provide the main productive assets, and accordingly they had little to offer lenders by way of collateral.

Administrator Black and representatives of all Northwest utilities rehashed these points at the JPPC's initial meeting in 1966. They were all agreed on a regional response to the near crisis of dwindling electrical reserves in the Bonneville system. BPA, unlike the Tennessee Valley Authority (which had already embarked on an ambitious thermal power development program), was not authorized to build generating facilities; it was up to the IOUs and PUDs to take power development into their own hands. BPA would, of course, continue to provide the basic transmission grid for all power, federal and non-federal, public and private. But it was this same interconnected network that had brought the utilities into interdependence, making the new watchwords of the energy future "one short, all short." The private and public competitors had been in a nip-and-tuck race for nearly three-quarters of a century, and in 1966 they were looking over their shoulders at the Juggernaut of political and economic necessity closing in behind them, gaining momentum with each passing year, its growing weight fed by population, new industry, anything that demands more power. It was time for the competitors to stop elbowing each other for the lead and to begin running in tandem to outdistance the Juggernaut, or get crushed together beneath blackouts, red ink, lawsuits, and bankruptcy. The region's utilities needed a united, comprehensive plan, and the JPPC was where that plan would take form.

Shortly after that first meeting, the major IOUs discussed the possibility of forming a consortium of utilities for the purpose of building a large thermal plant. The three largest PUDs—Snohomish, Grays Harbor, and Clark—were invited to join the consortium, but they declined, fearing that the companies were using the conciliatory spirit of the JPPC in an attempt to divide WPPSS. The PUDs reacted by forming the Public Power Council in November 1966 which acted as the representative of public power in planning deliberations of the JPPC. The PPC was the natural offspring of the publics' relationship with the JPPC; the 100 consumer-owned agencies of the Northwest knew that they were strong only when united, and they were determined to face the IOUs across the meeting table from a position of strength.

Like the Washington PUD Association and WPPSS, the PPC was an organization based on voluntary participation. It was governed by an executive committee of 12 members split evenly between cooperatives, municipalities, and PUDs. Later, the committee was expanded to include four members from each category. Eventually, all 110 of the Northwest's publicly owned utilities had membership in the PPC.

The emergence of yet another organization consolidating the efforts of public power would have seemed to indicate that the ties that bound the motley collection of publics together were never stronger. Once again, appearances were deceiving, for the private companies were driving a wedge between the PUDs in 1967 that almost succeeded in dividing the PUD Association against itself.

The IOUs saw their chance to break the unity of the publics with a scheme that involved the Centralia coal-fired thermal plant. Centralia was the first tangible product of the JPPC sessions; the council had concluded that the region's first cooperatively built thermal plant should also be its first coal-fired plant. The project was proposed by the Big Four regional IOUs: Pacific Power & Light, Washington Water Power, Puget Sound Power & Light, and Portland General Electric. Centralia was viewed as a good start for the JPPC's emerging joint hydrothermal program, because it would be located at the site of a large lignite mine at Centralia in western Washington, which gave it an excellent location with respect to nearby electricity markets in the Puget Sound area; this meant lower transmission cost. Coal was not a desirable fuel from an environmental point of view, but burning it in a power plant used a well-seasoned technology. Having been rebuffed by Snohomish and Grays Harbor PUDs in 1966, the IOUs that put together the Centralia plan found the same PUDs more receptive in early 1967. Snohomish signed into the project for an eight percent share, Grays Harbor for four percent. Tacoma and Seattle both went in for eight percent.

With the four largest PUDs signed on to provide the financial support that the IOUs had been needing, the companies were thus ready to make their move in the state legislature. Since the early 1960s, the IOUs had been gradually building a power base in the Washington statehouse, and by 1967 they had effective control of the majority vote. They therefore introduced a bill that would permit a group of utilities to build new thermal power facilities in Washington. The same right, however, was denied joint operating agencies such as WPPSS.

Ken Billington, the PUD Association director, knew that he couldn't stop the bill's passage, so he directed Jack Cluck to "pull the teeth" from the measure in order to assure that it did the least amount of damage to the PUDs. Instead, Cluck attempted to amend the measure so that it would actually be favorable to the PUD position, then went to the PUD directors to elicit their support of his amendments, despite Billington's warning that the legislature would never accept such amendments. Billington, realizing that the Supply System's ability to ever build another project was hanging in the balance, met head-on with his trusted attorney. He pointed out to Cluck that the bill had been introduced by the private-power lawyers and thus was a private-power bill with irredeemable characteristics. He said it wouldn't pass with Cluck's revisions, and ordered Cluck to drop them and concentrate on reducing the bill's "bad" points instead of adding "good" ones. Cluck refused and the PUD and municipal participants in the Centralia project backed him up, perhaps believing that WPPSS' construction powers were no longer necessary in light of JPPC-inspired cooperation. Other publics rallied behind Billington. The two sides of the PUD Association's board of directors squared off at a meeting and argued long and hard before finally taking a vote of 16-4 in favor of adopting Billington's recommendation. Cluck reluctantly changed his strategy and the bill passed, but it was left open to future amendments; in 1973, it was amended to include joint operating agencies as entities with the right to build thermal (including nuclear) plants.

Throughout 1967 and 1968, the JPPC met frequently to forge a master plan for the Northwest that would endure a decade. Ten years of coordinated utility power development may not sound like much, but it was seen as a monumental feat by the fractious utility leaders: "You could never get an agreement on a long-term program," said the power manager of BPA. At last, the ten-year Hydro-Thermal Power Program was unveiled. It sought to build seven thermal plants (two coal, five nuclear) at a cost of $2 billion. In organization, the HTPP placed Bonneville in the crucial coordinating role, fashioning incentives and organizing negotiations. The major incentive BPA provided to the publics was an innovative financing device called "net billing."

The most important economic problem of regional power development was securing financing for power plants. For most publics, this was a fact of life. But some of the larger municipals, such as Seattle, Tacoma, and Eugene, had invested in major hydro projects on their own. With their larger, more experienced staffs, together with well-established financing capability in the municipal bond market, they felt capable of managing thermal plants. They resisted BPA's leadership, feeling that their autonomy might be compromised by too great a degree of interdependence. Bonneville overcame the reluctance of the public agencies with net billing. Under net billing, publics participating in the purchase of a thermal plant have the higher thermal costs averaged with the lower BPA hydro system costs by Bonneville. A PUD, for example, would sell 100 MW of thermally generated power to BPA for 20 mill/kwh. BPA would "meld" this high-cost power with its cheaper, hydro-produced federal power (typically costing less than 2 mill/kwh to generate) to arrive at an intermediate cost of 7 mill/kwh, the wholesale rate that it charges when it sells the power back to the

PUD. Though Bonneville would never make a capital outlay for the thermal power, the effect of the net-billing procedure is to put the financial resources and equity of the federal system behind the preference customers in the planned thermal plant ventures.

But net billing, in order to be attractive enough to the publics, took the preference policy one step too far, as BPA and all its customers would discover too late. Perhaps it is more correct to say that Bonneville left out an extra step in the net-billing scheme, the one that would have removed from BPA's hydro contracts the obligation to deliver power to its preference customers on a "firm" basis.

> This means in particular that BPA is obliged to supply the total power... even if the thermal plant should produce no output at all. . . .In this manner, the public utility participant is insured by BPA against the failure of the thermal plant. If a thermal project turned out no power at all—what utilities call a "dry hole"—BPA wholesale power prices would be raised throughout the region to cover the costs. Accordingly, the costs would be shared among all buyers of the federal hydro resource, not just participating utilities, for whom a dry hole could prove catastrophic. Net billing was an offer too good to refuse. Of BPA's more than 100 preference customers, only the city of Tacoma did not take advantage of net billing.

Net billing had to be approved by the Appropriations Committee of Congress, but before that it was scrutinized by the White House Office of Management and Budget, which objected on the grounds that it seemed too much like a guarantee to bail out public utilities. The mastermind of the net-billing concept, Bonneville power manager Bernard Goldhammer, was criticized by the OMB officials, who asked, "What do you do if these plants don't get into operation? Who pays for them? Are you going to come back and ask for an appropriation to bail out the costs for a plant that's not operating for any reason? Why can't the utilities in the Northwest finance and go ahead with these plants? Why should Bonneville be underwriting and spreading out the cost of a dry hole?" Goldhammer then asked the congressional General Accounting Office for an advisory opinion on the legality and fiscal prudence of net billing. GAO responded that the procedure was permissible. Amazingly, neither the OMB nor the GAO consulted their experts in the field on the matter. Net billing eventually received its okay from the Appropriations Committee.

For all the synergy and accord that seemed to flow from the Hydro-Thermal Power Program, there was a foreboding undercurrent of discontent beneath the surface. Shortly after the HTPP had been finalized, the old suspicions and animosities that had divided public and private interests welled up anew, threatening to undo over two years of hard negotiations.

The IOUs were not pleased with net billing, preserving as it did the sacred cow of public-utility preference. But they realized that without net billing the publics wouldn't accept the HTPP, and the companies needed the program worse than the publics did. So the IOUs engaged in some behind the scenes efforts to undermine the legal foundations of WPPSS and all the other PUDs, so that the private utilities could seize control of the energy destiny of the Northwest once and for all. Private power surrogates still controlled the Washington legislature in 1969, and they struck there as they had in 1967. They introduced a bill that would gut the 1930 PUD law affecting public-utility district formation, and another bill that would cripple the publics' ability to issue revenue bonds. The measure represented a one-two punch that could effectively knock out the ongoing WPPSS plans for future thermal projects. The private-power lobbyists in Olympia figured that severely damaging the Supply System's construction capabilities and stopping new PUDs (and thus new publicly oriented JOAs) from forming would put popular pressure on the publics, making it imperative for them to renegotiate the HTPP to the advantage of the IOUs.

As in 1967, Ken Billington knew that he was helpless to stop the attack. After 30 years in the public power crusade, after watching public power in Washington flourish and mature, after seeing the failure of one attempt after another to destroy the PUDs, after sharing in the triumph of the completion of the world's largest nuclear power plant (a plant built by WPPSS), Billington foresaw this legislative push as the most serious threat yet to the crusade. For the first time ever, he sought the advice of a BPA administrator, who in 1969 was H. R. Richmond. Richmond suggested that Billington arrange a meeting between public and private power leaders at which each side could air its grievances. Billington was able to arrange the meeting, but he felt that it would be better if he didn't attend. He sent a message through his representatives, however, that there could be no joint ownership at Centralia if the private companies were to continue their frontal attack in the legislature. The meeting ended in stalemate, and the scene thus was set for a climactic showdown.

On the Monday following that meeting, a lobbyist from Puget Sound Power & Light called Billington to invite him to dinner with the presidents of three of the Northwest Big Four IOUs. PUD commissioners Ed Fischer and Ed Taylor (both were also directors on the

WPPSS board) were also invited. Before leaving for the inevitable confrontation, Billington considered his options. Private power had the PUDs over a barrel, there was no doubt about that. But the PUDs did have one potential advantage: time. The Hydro-Thermal Power Program had to be implemented soon or its precise schedule of plant construction would be thrown off. If the offending state legislation passed, and chances were it would, the PUDs might be able to organize a referendum effort that would tie up the bills until they could be voted on by referendum in state elections a year and a half away.

Billington arrived at the dinner with Fischer and Taylor. Their counterparts were Donald Frisbee, president of Pacific Power & Light; Wendall Satre, president of Washington Water Power; and Ralph Davis, president of PSP&L. Billington opened the evening's conversation by stating that prior to leaving Olympia he had met with Lars Nelson, master of the state Grange, and Joe Davis, president of the state Labor Council. Nelson and Smith, said Billington, would back the PUD Association all the way in opposition to the measures being pushed through the legislature by the power companies.

> And that means simply this: If any bill which damages the PUD law is passed by the legislature and signed by the governor, that legislation will be taken to the voters on a referendum, and this state will be locked in a private-public power fight for the next 18 months the like of which no person has ever seen. Even in the end, should the private power position be sustained by the voters, the Centralia plant will in the meantime go down the drain as a joint ownership project, and the Hydro-Thermal Power Plan will be a miserable failure.

Billington's ultimatum worked. The IOU chiefs agreed to rein in the legislative aggression, on the condition that the publics facilitate some changes in the law that would ease financing for the private utilities, as a means of offsetting the publicly biased HTPP. The evening went cordially after that, and in the course of breaking bread together the Northwest's power leaders broke from tradition and achieved a consensus on the future of private-public relations. They concluded that the bitter fighting had gone on long enough, that neither side was ever going to win a decisive advantage, that the well-being of coming generations of Northwesterners was in their hands, and that therefore they were responsible for coming to a decision on whether they were going to "sink or swim together."

The envoys from the two sides of the Northwest power wars made an informal peace pact that night, the Hydro-Thermal Power Program went ahead, Centralia was completed as the first jointly built and jointly owned thermal plant, and a new decade of cooperation coincided with the 1970s. There would still be rough spots in the road of coordination ahead, but the struggle between the two old enemies was essentially over. The crusade and the power trust had seen the Juggernaut coming and acknowledged that it could not be stopped; it couldn't even be slowed down. So, they had resolved to work together in order to stay a step ahead of it. They began by trying to define it, to identify it. They called the Juggernaut "large-scale technocratic institutions," "evolving institutionalized imperatives," and "regionally integrated financial organization structures." But they did not fully recognize the Juggernaut until it was too late, and only then did they realize that it was indeed their own creation.

The Juggernaut was WPPSS.

# 6

# THE CONSTRUCTION PROGRAM

When Owen Hurd answered the phone on the afternoon of January 27, 1971, he was hoping that the call would be from the airline, confirming his flight reservations from Pasco to Olympia the next day. It was a trip he looked forward to, for the occasion that was taking him to Olympia was a gala presentation dinner, at which state officials and public power leaders would gather. The highlight of the evening's celebration was to be the presentation of a $25,000 site certification application fee to the state from WPPSS, for the privilege of beginning work on WPPSS's first totally consumer-owned nuclear power plant, Hanford No. 2. It would mark a high point in the 14-year history of the Supply System, and observe the start of a new energy era for the agency and for Washington. After all the work he had put in over the previous three weeks coordinating the complex financial and contractual arrangements between WPPSS, the 94 underwriting utilities, and BPA, Hurd was ready for a little fun.

The man on the other end of the phone said that he was John Ehrlichman calling from the White House. For a second, Hurd sorted out possibilities in his mind: Was the guy actually calling from *the* White House? If not *the* White House, then which one? Hurd had been to the White House, had even shook hands with the president. But that had been back in 1962, when Hurd had attended the signing of the Hanford NPR-steam plant authorization bill in the Oval Office, after which he received the signature pen and a handshake from Kennedy. Hurd hadn't even thought about the White House much since then. But here was this Ehrlichman, whom Hurd had never heard of, telling him that at 5:01 p.m. the next day, Hurd was to shut down the NPR reactor at Hanford for good.

This was too much for the managing director of the Supply System. "Who says so?" he demanded. "The president's budget says so," replied John Ehrlichman.

In the next few hours, Hurd tried desperately to sort out what was happening. The order to switch off the Hanford reactor had come so totally out of the blue that he wasn't even sure he had the authority to follow the White House directive. What he found out was that the presidential budget for fiscal 1971 did not include funds for the plutonium-producing reactor at Hanford, known by 1971 as the "N-reactor." The eight other reactors at Hanford had been shut down one by one in the late 1960s as the international arms race had cooled. Hurd had been aware that the Nixon Administration had been cutting down drastically on plutonium production at the remaining reactor because of recent arms agreements between the United States and the Soviet Union. But he couldn't believe that there wasn't someone in the administration who realized how important the N-reactor was in terms of the region's energy availability.

By the next morning, the Tri-Cities were already mobilizing in reaction to the N-reactor shutdown scheduled for that evening. Civic leaders estimated that almost half of the jobs in the Tri-Cities area would be wiped out by the shutdown. Scoop Jackson warned that it could lead to a loss of 7,500 jobs in the Northwest. The local AFL-CIO appealed to national labor leader George Meany to put pressure on the administration until it changed its directive. Charles Bovers, the chairman of Douglas United Nuclear, a Hanford scientific firm, said the shutdown's meaning for Richland was "the beginning of a ghost town." Owen Hurd charged the AEC with violating its contract with WPPSS, which stated that negotiations between the government and the Supply System would precede significant change in the N-reactor's operation. He said that the shutdown wiped out the reserve generating capacity of the region, threatening brownouts across the Northwest. The *Tri-City Herald* discovered in the course of conversations with government officials that the deactivation of the N-reactor was aimed at saving the government $45 million in long-term costs. The decision to exclude funds, according to John Ehrlichman, had been made by a deputy director of the Office of Management and Budget named Caspar Weinberger.

That evening, the mood at the presentation dinner was weighted with the day's events. Providing some relief was the moment when

Ed Taylor, president of the WPPSS executive committee, presented an application to build Hanford No. 2 to the chairman of the state Power Siting Council, along with a check for $25,000, the normal fee for site certification. Following the presentation, Governor Dan Evans announced that he would fly to Washington, D.C., in a few days to head a fight for government funds necessary to operate the N-reactor.

When Evans and other officials from the state and from WPPSS arrived in the nation's capital, the AEC announced it was suspending the shutdown of the N-reactor in order to allow Washington state officials to state their case. Personnel reductions were deferred, and the Tri-Cities breathed a little easier as the danger of mass unemployment was postponed.

The representatives from the Nixon Administration who met with the Evans contingent were blunt. The N-reactor was "unreliable and a possible safety hazard," they said. It did not meet AEC standards for commercial reactors, and they stated that it would cost millions of dollars to bring it up to those standards. They called the reactor a "sloppy engineering job." The WPPSS engineers who had come to defend the reactor admitted that it had experienced many problems in its first few years of operation, and that it had taken them an unusually long time to get the bugs out of the system. But, they assured the president's men, they had overcome most of the technical problems; the reactor had run at maximum capacity for most of 1970, a record almost as good as the U.S. average for commercial nuclear plants. Donald B. Rice, assistant director of the OMB, was not impressed. "After allowing for likely net payments for steam and for the value of plutonium produced," he said, "the AEC would still be out $20 million a year." He suggested that WPPSS, in concert with state people from Olympia, come up with an acceptable plan; otherwise, the N-reactor would be put out to pasture with its eight predecessors at Hanford.

The threat to shut down the N-reactor posed the first significant problem for the Hydro-Thermal Power Program, which had been officially launched only a month before, on January 1, 1971. By that time, WPPSS had already been granted a key role in carrying out the objectives of the HTPP. It was a role that the Supply System may well have coveted and did indeed actively seek.

A few months after the Joint Power Planning Council was formed in October 1966, WPPSS began studying the possibility of building its own nuclear power plant. The Hanford Generating Project had been completed the previous year, and the Supply System was anxious to make use of its newly acquired engineering and financing expertise toward another thermal project. In early 1967, WPPSS sent a proposal to the Public Power Council and Bonneville, stating its readiness to undertake construction of a 1,000-MW nuclear power plant to meet regional needs. Even before the two planning agencies replied, the WPPSS board approved Hurd's recommendation of Westinghouse as supplier of the plant's turbo-generator, and authorized Hurd to obtain bids for a nuclear steam supply system. The board was betting that the JPPC was going to conclude that at least one nuclear plant was in the region's future. WPPSS was going to be more than ready to take on the job.

The PPC then came up with a plan that represented the regional public agencies' participation in the evolving HTPP. Along with a 28 percent interest in Centralia, public power would have a 30 percent portion of a nuclear plant that Portland General Electric was building on the Oregon side of the lower Columbia. The publics' power from the PGE plant (called Trojan) would be net billed. The PPC also included in its plan a 100 percent net-billed, 1,100-MW, "unidentified" nuclear plant, to be built by a public utility in either Oregon or Washington. It was agreed that the Eugene Water & Electric Board (EWEB), the municipal of the Oregon city, would have the plant built somewhere in Oregon by late 1974. WPPSS would begin building the next publicly owned nuclear plant a year after EWEB began construction, so that the WPPSS plant would be ready for start-up in late 1975. A contingency plan was also prepared, whereby should EWEB be unable for any reason to begin construction as scheduled, the Supply System would then immediately start building its plant.

EWEB spent a year exploring potential sites around western Oregon. One of the more promising locales was an area north of Florence, on the central Oregon coast. On April 15, 1970, the residents of Florence unanimously signed a petition to Governor Tom McCall favoring construction of the nuclear plant in their back yard. It was a fine show of community solidarity; McCall, however, had no jurisdiction over the siting of power projects. Florentines and other local nuclear enthusiasts must have been disappointed by what happened next in Eugene. There, on May 26, the city's voters decided that EWEB should delay further siting studies for four years. The initiative effectively halted Eugene's part in the regional plant construction program, and handed the sponsorship of public power's first nuclear plant over to WPPSS. With EWEB out of the nuclear picture for awhile, the PPC asked WPPSS to go ahead with construction of its planned nuclear plant. On July 17, the WPPSS board of directors authorized application to the AEC for a construction permit. By this time they had chosen as the most promising site Roosevelt Beach, in Grays Harbor County on the central Washington coast (by coincidence, the EWEB site on the central Oregon coast was within a mile of a town which was also called Roosevelt Beach). A plan had also been made for a second nuclear power plant at Hanford. The Roosevelt Beach plant was given a planned completion date of September 1977, and the Hanford plant's completion was scheduled for a year after that.

The next step was to sign on an architect-engineer, the firm that would do the designing work for the plant. After three months of research, a task force of WPPSS staff recommended Burns & Roe as the AE for the plant. At a meeting of the board of directors on October 14, WPPSS approved a contract of $14 million to Burns & Roe. This was to be the first major expenditure of an anticipated total cost of $400 million for the plant, up from the $352 million estimate given when it was listed as one of the seven original plants in the Hydro-Thermal Program in 1969. Another crucial decision made by the WPPSS board was the one on the site location for the project. Fears had been expressed by the PPC that Roosevelt Beach might leave the project licensing process open to intervenors and thus delay the construction start. Hanford was friendly territory, already proud of its heritage of atomic power and the Supply System's role there; the site for the first WPPSS nuclear construction project, it was decided, should be Hanford. The project was simply called Hanford No. 2.

The meeting of October 14, 1970, represented a turning point for WPPSS. At that meeting it acknowledged its responsibility as an emerging energy leader in the Northwest, with all the attendant managerial tasks and functions. In response to this, the directors of WPPSS voted to restructure their organization through the creation of an executive committee of not more than seven members. The committee would meet frequently to carry out projects approved by the 18-member board of directors. The board would meet quarterly to receive committee reports, give direction, and approve budgets and new projects.

In June 1970 when the PPC asked WPPSS to begin its construction schedule, the permanent staff of the Supply System numbered 66. Only six months later, with its Hanford No. 2 project moving ahead, that staff was approaching 100. Snohomish's William G. Hulbert, who had joined the executive committee for the first time in September, was appalled at a problem with which he would become all too familiar in years to come. Requests for more staff and more salary, he said, were getting out of hand. He criticized "costly and time-consuming" investigations into Canadian coal resources ("a dead-end street," he said) and work on a demonstration breeder reactor ("a hole in our pocket"). He ventured that the "whole nation, including environmentalists, is watching to see how well a public agency can perform. . . . We must concentrate on Hanford No. 2. It is on our shoulders to get this built on time."

At the beginning of 1971, WPPSS signed net-billing contracts with BPA to guarantee $15 million in interim financing for the $400 million Hanford No. 2 plant. The money was coming from revenue bonds issued by 94 consumer-owned utilities throughout Bonneville's service area. To afford oversight to these underwriting utilities, BPA organized the Participants Review Board of representatives from the 94 participating publics. Most of these "participants," as they were called, were not member-owners of the Supply System. The direct member utilities of WPPSS had by this time increased to 19 PUDs. On May 19, 1967, the city of Richland became the first municipal light system to join the Supply System as a full member. Seattle City Light joined on March 23, 1971. At that time, WPPSS was in the middle of negotiations with the OMB, the AEC, the Interior Department, and the state of Washington regarding the future of the N-reactor.

Agreement was reached by all parties on March 31. The AEC would continue to operate the reactor for the next three years provided that WPPSS paid the commission a maximum of $20 million a year for the privilege of having access to the reactor's waste heat. The OMB then gave WPPSS until June 30, 1972, to decide on whether it wanted to exercise the contractual provision of assuming full responsibility for the reactor's operation.

The Supply System's engineers did a year of intensive studies on the N-reactor. In May 1972 they informed the PPC that converting the N-reactor to a power-only mode of operation was impractical. Therefore, in order to settle the remaining contractual rights of the private companies which owned a 50 percent share of the reactor's power, WPPSS announced that it planned to add a high-pressure topping turbine to the existing generating plant. Simultaneously, it planned to also begin construction on a new reactor to eventually take the place of the N-reactor, to be called Hanford No. 1. The idea was to continue to use the existing generating plant, but to gradually phase out the old N-reactor with a new nuclear steam supply system. The whole package was scheduled for completion in September 1980. The PPC as a whole liked the idea, but there were some members on its board from utilities west of the cascades who expressed concern about concentrating all the plant construction at Hanford. Most of the region's future power needs would be on their side of the mountains, they pointed out, and transmitting electricity all the way from the lower eastern corner of Washington was going to be costly. They wanted the next power plant to be located close to the population centers in the Puget Sound-Willamette Valley corridor, which stretched in a band of cities and towns from northern Washington to southern Oregon. The Supply System was supposed to be a decentralized agency, the western publics complained, yet they had clustered all three publicly operated thermal plants at their power base in the Tri-Cities. In order to move ahead with Hanford No. 1, the PPC came to a consensus on a concurrent call for another nuclear plant to be built by WPPSS in western Washington. It asked the Supply System if it could begin construction on this plant, dubbed simply No. 3, shortly after it started on Hanford No. 1. The WPPSS executive committee rose to the challenge in its unanimous assent.

Virtually overnight the Supply System had taken on two more nuclear construction programs in addition to one that was just barely getting under way. And, only a few months later, additional studies of Hanford No. 1 showed that the project's objectives of adding and rebuilding around the existing generators would be "too complex." WPPSS instead revised the project into one in which an entire 1,250-MW nuclear power system would be built in another area of the Hanford reservation, leaving the HGP/N-reactor system as it was. (For the sake of simplicity, the names of all the projects were officially set in December 1972 as follows: Hanford No. 1 became WNP-1, Hanford No. 2 was changed to WNP-2, Project No. 3 became WNP-3, and the HGP/N-reactor plant became known simply as Hanford. Most utility people called them WPPSS No. 1, WPPSS No. 2, etc., or simply No. 1 and No. 2.) No. 1 had grown from a power-enhancement scheme at an existing plant as a means of meeting contract obligations, to a separate and complete nuclear project. No. 3 had been used as a means of getting all members of the PPC to authorize No. 1. Of course, these were not the only reasons that the projects were started, nor were the PPC and WPPSS the only entities involved in authorizing them. The plants were given the blessings of the IOUs, BPA, the state of Washington, the Northwest Public Power Association, the Washington PUD Association, a dozen other regional organizations and, eventually, the AEC. All were deeply concerned about the growing electricity needs of the region. All were convinced that nuclear energy was the most economical answer to those needs. There was not a single doubt expressed by any power-planning group that those three WPPSS plants would not all be needed even before their scheduled commercial operation dates.

Still, the Supply System in a short period of time was faced with a construction budget that had trebled from $500 million to over $1.6 billion. But the new managing director who took over from the retiring Owen Hurd in 1972 was particularly well known for his ability to handle budgets. J. J. Stein had run a tight ship as the manager of Grays Harbor PUD since 1954, which was not surprising, since he had skippered a destroyer during the war. He had cut his engineering teeth at Puget Sound Power & Light before switching over to the public-power side, where he made his mark as an organizer. Stein in 1972 inherited a just-born yet full-blown nuclear power program, so his organizing abilities were put to the test from his first day on the job. He had no nuclear engineering experience—experienced nuclear engineers were scarce in those days, when commercial nuclear power was only a few steps past getting its feet wet—but he had confidence in his rapidly growing staff, and in October of 1972 he summed up his first status report as follows:

> While our overnight growth has been a shock, it has not been traumatic. The reason is that initially we were able to secure some well-qualified, dedicated young engineers to undertake the Hanford Number Two Project. We now have people with more than 265 man-hours of nuclear experience on the staff and we are prepared to carry out the challenge of getting these three plants on line in time to meet the area power requirements.

With former-Captain Stein providing a steady hand at the helm, and net billing smoothing the economic waves before it, the Supply System appeared to be steering the right course.

However, net billing hit a snag in 1972, when a new federal tax ruling removed government agencies from "exempt" status in the use of tax-exempt municipal bonds; thus any direct "sales" of power to BPA would henceforth require financing by taxable bonds. The ruling sharply limited the possibilities of cooperative plant investments between public and investor-owned utilities, investments which were net billing's raison d'être. But an even greater difficulty for net billing was the skyrocketing cost of the Hydro-Thermal Power Program. The capital needed to build HTPP's thermal plants was rapidly exceeding the supply that could be backed by net billing. Early in 1973, BPA estimated that by 1981 the revenues derived from the sale of federal hydro to preference customers would amount to $145 million. But the annual cost of the thermal plants built under HTPP by 1981 would have mounted to $135 million, over the net billing limit of 85 percent.

The soaring costs of the WPPSS construction program would become the major headache for Stein and his successors, but for Stein they were particularly frustrating. As Grays Harbor manager, he had prided himself in his ability to "hold the line" on utility operating and construction costs.

He was aware that a nuclear plant was "a whole different beast" as engineers liked to phrase it, but what he—and all utility people in the country, as it became apparent—had not anticipated was that the beast was continually changing. New regulations were issued by the AEC that required significant changes in the designs of nuclear plants being planned or built across the nation. The design changes and the construction delays that they caused added costs to these projects. As early as December 1971 BPA administrator H. R. Richmond warned that delays in the schedules of power-generating projects were threatening the integrity of the HTPP. A year later, the changes and resultant delays in the WNP-2 project necessitated drastic revisions in estimates of total costs and construction time. The cost of No. 2 was reset from $400 million to $504 million, and the scheduled commercial operation date, or COD, was changed from September 1977 to September 1978. The CODs for WNP-1 and WNP-3 were each also moved forward in time, or "slipped," a year.

Richmond retired on December 1, 1972, and his deputy administrator Don Hodel immediately took over. Hodel's appointment to BPA chief was welcomed by utility people in the Northwest who were concerned about Richmond's leadership abilities in what was rapidly becoming a desperate regional situation. Russ Richmond had been the first BPA career man to rise through the ranks to the administrator's position where he inevitably adopted the settled style of a lifetime bureaucrat at the brink of retirement. Hodel was expected to bring fresh ideas along with new blood to the agency, the way that Chuck Luce had in the 1960s. Like Luce, Hodel was relatively young, polished, and dynamic, with a background in law.

The first two weeks in his new administrator's post were a baptism of fire and ice for Hodel. A prolonged cold spell caused major power supply problems and forced drastic curtailments of BPA service to its direct-service industrial customers. Hodel bluntly predicted that the power crisis was merely a taste of things to come, and added:

> It is therefore mandatory that we estimate effective procedures for cop-
> ing with the power shortages which face us during the next few years....
> Most importantly, the cooperative regional Hydro-Thermal Power Pro-
> gram must be continued. . .Unfortunately, it appears that the net-bill-
> ing procedure adopted by Bonneville to help finance non-Federal ther-
> mal power plants will no longer be feasible after fiscal year 1982. . . .It
> is hoped that a solution will be found and found soon to keep the
> unique Hydro-Thermal Power Program viable because the economic life
> and well-being of the entire region are at stake.

The next year, 1973, marked a major shift in the HTPP. Hodel
called representatives of BPA, the region's IOUs, publics, and direct-
service industries (DSIs) together in January and informed them that
the HTPP was not working. At the heart of its problems was the heart
of the program: net billing. The informal council of utility people
agreed that net billing was woefully inadequate as the economic engine to drive construction of additional thermal plants. Thus net billing, which had been put into effect in 1971 and was supposed to carry
the program to 1981, was scrapped after only two years. The WPPSS
plants would continue to be built with net-billed financing, but future
plants would require a different approach.

Power planners in 1973 acknowledged that the Northwest was
going to be in deep trouble in the 1980s unless some more generating
plants were built. Forecasts done by the Pacific Northwest Utilities
Conference Committee predicted that loads would continue to grow
at between five and seven percent a year for the next ten years. Even
if all the HTPP's thermal plants were completed on time (a questionable prospect), the PNUCC reports indicated, energy demand would
begin to exceed supply by the end of 1982. After that, according to
PNUCC, the region would move rapidly into a situation of mass
energy deficits. Based on these forecasts, Hodel informed the IOUs
that they would no longer be able to receive new power contracts
after their current ones expired. The reason was because the Preference Policy obliged BPA to place priority on its contracts with its
preference customers, the publics, and after 1982, Bonneville could
reasonably ensure that there would be only enough power for its
preference customers. Later in 1973, even that assumption would be
in jeopardy.

The prospect of an end to access to firm federal power must have
been devastating to the IOUs, even if they were expecting it. For the
DSIs, the future looked even worse, because they relied completely
on BPA for their electricity. And, most of the DSIs were aluminum

companies, which are energy-intensive industries; therefore, the chances of the DSIs finding another utility source for their huge electrical needs were next to zero. The DSIs complained that they were victims of the region's hydroelectric heritage; for almost 30 years they had been buying excess electricity from the BPA system at lower than wholesale cost. The surplus power was cheap because it was "interruptible." That is, it was whatever power was left of that used by the preference customers and the contracted IOUs. This had been a tolerable situation for the DSIs because it rendered them the cheapest electricity in the world. Until the late 1960s, it had seemed that the margin of hydroelectricity would always be there for the benefit of the DSIs. In 1973, it was beginning to look like there soon wouldn't be enough available energy for the aluminum companies to turn out a single beer can.

Throughout 1973, the region's utility leaders and planners brainstormed in meetings at Bonneville's headquarters in Portland, pounding out a new framework for the faltering HTPP. On December 14, 1973, Hodel announced the completion of the new plan. The net-billing portion of the HTPP was given the label of Phase I and officially declared ended. The WPPSS plants would continue to be net-billed as Phase I plants. Phase II of the Hydro-Thermal Program would begin as soon as it was approved by the Secretary of the Interior. In place of net billing, a direct financing by the utilities, without BPA backing, would be employed to build additional thermal plants. The utilities had agreed to build ten more jointly owned thermal plants by 1991. The first two plants on the Phase II construction agenda were to be nuclear, and they were to be built by WPPSS.

The decision to have the Supply System add two more nuclear plants to its already ambitious construction program was widely criticized in later years, but in December of 1973 it had the unanimous support of the region's utilities. The major impetus, aside from the widely held perception of need, was a concept known as "twinning": building a duplicate of a nuclear unit already under construction on the same site. Costs of siting and licensing would conceivably be saved, and some construction costs would, theoretically, be "shared." The idea had worked quite well at a few nuclear projects around the country. The power planners reasoned that building two separate nuclear units—or even one unit and its "twin"—would be more expensive than adding twins (technically known as "second units") to the nuclear plants already under construction. Since the Supply System was sponsoring those units, it was obvious that it should also oversee the Phase

II units; to have a different utility heading the twin-unit projects would have surely led to confusion and friction. Therefore, WPPSS was designated to manage the construction and financing of the projects.

The problem, then, was financing the additional plants. The formulators of Phase II came up with a fiscal replacement for net billing known as a "participants' agreement." Each utility that signed such an agreement would be participating in a project by taking a portion of the project's debt in exchange for a respective share of the plant's output. The difference between the Participants' Agreements for the Phase II plants and the underwriting contracts that public utilities had signed for WNP-1, 2, and 3 was that participants in Nos. 1-3 were not directly responsible for the projects' debts. The Participants' Agreements had the effect of cutting out BPA as the power broker with ultimate responsibility for paying off borrowed construction funds and associated debt interest.

In early 1974, the Public Power Council, acting on behalf of the region's advocates of Phase II, asked the Supply System to build two more nuclear units. On May 29, 1974, WPPSS formally accepted the task. Since WNP-2 was too far along in construction to be "twinned" with significant cost-saving effects, the second units were designated for projects 1 and 3. WNP-4 would be built at the No. 1 site, and WNP-5 would be built alongside No. 3. As designing and licensing efforts got under way for the two second units, a simultaneous endeavor began in order to sign up participants for 4 and 5.

The IOUs agreed to take a 30 percent ownership of No. 5, as they had for its "twin," WNP-3. WPPSS then turned to the region's 110 publicly owned utilities to back No. 4 100 percent, and to take the remaining share of WNP-5. By this time, all of these publics had signed the underwriting contracts for Nos. 1-3, but they balked at signing the Participants' Agreements because the agreements were not backed by Bonneville. And WPPSS financial consultants on Wall Street said that the 4 and 5 revenue bonds would carry a higher rate of interest on return than the 1, 2, and 3 bonds. However, the consultants added that it was natural for the 4/5 bonds to have higher interest rates because investors in the bond market viewed those bonds, which lacked federal backing, as having greater risk than bonds on WNP 1, 2, and 3. Consequently, investors had to be motivated by higher interest rates in order to secure bond sales. Yet, according to the WPPSS Wall Street contacts, more attractive interest rates were not enough to assure that the bonds would be sold.

The Supply System's financial consultants at that time were Blyth Eastman, Paine, Webber, Inc., and Wood & Dawson, two nationally renowned New York investment firms. Paine Webber assured WPPSS that the 4/5 bonds would have no trouble selling on Wall Street and across the country if the Participants' Agreements were appropriately formulated. Yet as early as 1974 some brokerage houses had expressed concern about a possible saturation of the market with WPPSS bonds. By that time, the Supply System had issued only $105 million in revenue bonds, all of which sold quickly. But one report, written by a Merrill Lynch analyst, pointed out that WPPSS planned to issue over $1.5 billion more in bonds to finance its first three plants. The report warned that, should WPPSS go ahead with plans for plants 4 and 5, the market might not be able to absorb the additional $1 billion in cumulative WPPSS bond sales. The reports' author was immediately threatened with an industry "blackball" by Donald Patterson, Blyth Eastman's senior executive assigned to the Supply System, and the report was squelched. However, the fears expressed in the report had already made Wall Street jittery about any Supply System bonds not backed by BPA's net-billing arrangement. Therefore, Blyth Eastman recommended that the Participants' Agreements contain adequate compensation for the lack of "gilt-edging" that federal backing had given to WNP-1, 2, and 3 bonds. Almost buried amid the fiscal and legal jargon of each contract was a phrase which stipulated that the signing utility was obligated to pay for its designated share of WNP 4/5, *regardless of whether the plants were ever completed.* The phrase was later to become famous around the Northwest as the "hell or high water" clause.

By mid-1974, the Participants' Agreements were ready for signing, and a handful of publics had agreed to buy into 4 and 5. But many were still reluctant. Thus began a concerted effort by BPA, WPPSS, and the IOUs to put pressure on the publics to sign the contracts. Hodel wrote personal letters to the commissioners of every PUD in the region, urging them to participate in 4/5 ownership for the sake of the Northwest's future well-being. Most commissioners ignored the call. The BPA administrator sent his area managers to the offices of the PUDs, municipals, and rural co-ops to make a pitch for 4 and 5 and the agreements.

The area managers, in presenting their position, relied heavily on the PNUCC forecasts of electricity shortages in the mid-1980s unless 4 and 5 were built. But the forecasts were widely deemed as unreliable. (The following year, PNUCC did a public opinion survey which showed that its forecasts of the need for power were declining in credibility, with half the populace of the Northwest refusing to believe in a future shortage of electricity. Support for nuclear power, the first choice of 38 percent of the sample, was declining from its position of previous years.) Even after the PPC, the Washington PUD Association, and the Northwest Public Power Association (all of them supposedly representative organizations of publicly owned utilities' interest) had pleaded with the publics to sign the agreements, most of them still refused. Public hearings were held throughout the region in which delegates from the various power agencies stated their case, but the majority of Northwesterners were skeptical, and the public utilities they owned reflected this skepticism.

Meanwhile, as with Phase I, the heart of the problem was financial arrangements. Phase II was faltering. In 1975, Alumax, a direct-service industrial customer of BPA, bowed to environmentalist pressure in deciding to change the site of its proposed aluminum plant from Warrenton, Oregon, to Umatilla, in eastern Oregon. As a condition of shifting the point of delivery, Bonneville asked Alumax to sign one of the new, Phase II, 20-year contracts. These so-called IF-1 contracts transferred a part of the unexpected financial burden of the Phase I plants to the DSIs. A group of businessmen in Astoria, angered that the economic benefits from the proposed Alumax plant were being transferred away from nearby Warrenton, filed suit, naming Hodel as defendant. *Port of Astoria* v. *Hodel* turned on whether the Alumax contract for IF-1 power constituted a major federal action requiring a full-scale environmental impact statement (EIS). The U.S. District Court for Oregon ruled that BPA could not continue its collaborative power policy efforts with the region's utilities until an adequate EIS, explicitly defining BPA's role in the Northwest power supply system, was completed. This document came to be known as the Role EIS. Shortly after *Port of Astoria* was filed, the Natural Resources Defense Council, an environmentalist group based in San Francisco, also sued Hodel to seek the relief that was ultimately granted in the Role EIS. The embattled BPA administrator struck back in a speech in July, referring to environmentalists as "prophets of shortage" whose "theater of operations is the courtroom, where they are always the plaintiff, . . . seldom winning a case but satisfied to keep progress at bay with their legal maneuvers."

By late spring of 1976, Hodel was under an extraordinary amount of pressure, from WPPSS, the WPPSS Wall Street consultants, the IOUs, and the DSIs to do something to convince the publicly owned utilities to sign for WNP-4/5. The Hydro-Thermal Power Program was in serious trouble, with Phase II effectively halted pending completion of the Role EIS, which would take years to document. BPA was also faring poorly; for the third fiscal year in a row, the agency was operating in the red, and the deficit was growing larger each year. Bonneville had taken the controversial but necessary step the previous year of substantially increasing its wholesale rates, but the hike was offset by lower than expected revenues, and additional increases in the near future were out of the question. BPA's highly touted energy research projects were in jeopardy because of budget constraints. And, of course, the schedule slippages in the Phase I projects meant that BPA would have to wait that much longer for the revenue that would come from those projects' electricity sales, dragging deficits out still further.

Meanwhile, WPPSS Projects 4 and 5, which had been approved by power planners (including those from the PPC) in 1973, were essentially complete in design and had gone through all the site hearings. The project engineering teams were awaiting the go-ahead, and simply retaining them while 4/5 remained on hold was expensive. But the Supply System's Wall Street consultants advised that loans to extend the preconstruction phase of the projects would be increasingly hard to get unless some progress on signing of the agreements was made. Construction work would have to start soon, they warned, or the projects should be allowed to die on the vine. This prospect fomented some resentment at WPPSS, BPA, and the corporate headquarters of the Big Four IOUs, all of which had had a part in cranking out a mountain of studies for the design and licensing of 4 and 5. It was a resentment directed at the publics, which seemed to be standing alone in the way of the region's energy growth. The publics, on the other hand, tended to focus on the other realities of their signing of the Participants' Agreements, which even the advocates of WNP-4/5 admitted to: higher electric rates throughout the Northwest, PUDs and municipals in debt for 30 years, and tiny electrical co-ops saddled with project ownership responsibilities totally new to them.

The debate had come to an impasse in June 1976. Breaking the deadlock would require an extraordinary move, and Don Hodel initiated it by issuing a "notice of power insufficiency" to BPA's customers throughout the region. The notice informed the customers that Bonneville could no longer guarantee that sufficient power would be available for their needs after 1982. At best, the notice of insufficiency was premature until more sophisticated forecasts could be made to corroborate those of PNUCC. At worst, it was tantamount to a threat to the public-utility holdouts to sign the Participants' Agreements or risk brownouts, if not blackouts, seven years hence. The warning from BPA raised a few eyebrows; after all, the nation was supposedly still in the midst of an energy crisis. And it was not unexpected. Hodel had been given the authority to issue the notice back in 1973, when Interior Secretary Rogers Morton instructed the BPA administrator to "informally" notify "all BPA customers that notices of power insufficiency. . .would be issued. . .unless the utilities and BPA develop a plan for carrying forward the [HTPP] or some alternative procedure which would assure the region of a future power supply and minimize financial demands on the Federal Treasury." Ever since that 1973 notification, the question in the backs of minds throughout the region's utilities had not been *whether* Hodel would issue the notice, but *when*.

The issuance of the notice of insufficiency worked. Within a month, the total number of publics signed into ownership shares of 4/5 had risen to 88. The two notable nonparticipants were the cities of Seattle and Eugene.

Almost as meaningful to the publics as the notice of insufficiency was a letter sent to each utility by Governor Evans, endorsing the necessity of WNP-4 and 5. Dan Evans was widely respected in Washington as a very intelligent, extremely capable, and highly fair-minded administrator. His support of 4 and 5 may have swung several reluctant utilities into participation. Ironically, Evans would play a pivotal role in killing the same projects nearly seven years later. Long before that, the Hydro-Thermal Power Program would be in shambles, BPA's rates would be soaring, the Northwest's rate payers would be enraged into unprecedented activism, and the Participants' Agreements would be rent by legal mutiny. No one foresaw these events in July 1976, and so the 88 signers of the agreements proceeded to seal their fates with that of WPPSS. Even as they signed, unknown to them, the Supply System was careening with increasing momentum toward disaster.

# 7

# NUCLEAR BOOM YEARS

At the time that WPPSS was filing its applications for WNP-3, with the state and with the AEC, a nationwide scramble was on by utilities large and small for nuclear engineering services, nuclear consultants, and nuclear plant equipment. The driving factor was a widely held apprehension of an impending "energy crisis," which was depicted in a variety of scenarios of the time ranging between irritating inconvenience and post-industrial apocalypse. Popular acknowledgment of the "crisis" accelerated during the Arab oil embargo following the Yom Kippur War in the Middle East in October 1973. For industries, businesses, and residences which relied on oil for space and water heating, the oil shortage and severe price increases accompanying the embargo's end were a clear signal to switch to electricity in order to avoid soaring fuel costs. The nation's electric utilities viewed the sharp escalation in electricity demand as a long-term trend, and so expedited plans for new thermal plants. Many of these plants were coal-fired, but coal, though abundant in some parts of the United States had limitations: it was expensive and dangerous to mine, and environmentally malignant in every stage of its procurement, consumption, and waste disposal processes. Nuclear power also had drawbacks, but it was considered the best alternative in the many cases for which coal-fueled energy was inappropriate.

There were 35 nuclear plants in commercial operation in the United States at the end of 1973; it was still a relatively young and inexperienced technology, but the utilities were satisfied that questions regarding its safety and environmental effects were minor and solvable. Consequently, no less than 120 nuclear power projects were on the drawing boards in 1973 and 1974. As a result of this "nuclear boom," there was a growing scarcity of qualified engineering personnel in the handful of national architectural-engineering firms dealing in nuclear plant design. At the time the Public Power Council requested the Supply System to commence WNP-3, the first choice of WPPSS for No. 3 architect-engineer was Burns & Roe, which had been the AE for the Hanford Generating Project and therefore was chosen next to design WNP-2. However, Burns & Roe was stretched to its limit and could not undertake the No. 3 project. Therefore, after a period of reviewing proposals from other AEs, WPPSS selected Ebasco as the designer for 3. At about the same time, Bonneville was completing its study of the proposed retrofit of the HGP. By law, BPA had oversight of the HGP's budgets and had retained United Engineers & Constructors for its study. When the decision was made to abandon the retrofit and opt for the route that evolved into the WNP-1 project, it was logical that the architectural-engineering work should be left with UE&C. Thus, the Supply System in 1973 wound up largely through happenstance with three different firms designing three different nuclear power plants. Twinning plants 1 and 3 in 1974 extended the work of those projects' AEs to 4 and 5.

WPPSS encountered somewhat the same problem in ordering reactors for its plants. Utilities across the nation were jostling to get a place in the line that had formed for reactor orders, and therefore each usually ordered the first reactor to become available, in order to avoid construction schedule slippages. The Supply System was no exception, but it had another constraint to deal with. The PUD law, which applied to public joint operating agencies, required that bids be obtained on all construction and equipment contracts, with the award going to the lowest qualified bidder. WPPSS recognized that designating a particular type of reactor for its plants would have risked raising a legal challenge to its adherence to the PUD law. These two factors, nationwide competition for reactor supplies and mandatory competitive bidding requirements, combined to result in WPPSS's unenviable situation of having three different types of reactors from three suppliers in its five units. If that were not enough, WNP-2 had a reactor process distinct from its four successors; its process used a boiling-water reactor, while Plants 1, 2, 4, and 5 used pressurized-water reactors. The dissimilarities in equipment precluded any possibilities of WPPSS sharing materials between plants in case of spot parts shortages or termination of one or two projects.

These divergences and multiplicities in AE firms, plant designs, reactor types, process types, and equipment suppliers added up to a monumental challenge for WPPSS management. To add to the confusion, the Supply System's obligation to competitive bidding on its contracts resulted in a situation in which it had to keep track of hundreds of contracts from over a hundred contractors. Furthermore, any contract changes of over $25,000 above the contract's bid estimate had to have the approval of the full board of directors, again according to state law. As early as 1974, such substantial contract changes were becoming so common that the board was approving them without more than a glance at the reasons for the revisions; more thorough review would take too much time and hold up the projects. Before long, contracts that added *less* than $25,000 to the bid estimate were the exception.

Another recurring problem was peculiar to labor contractors. In early 1974, a labor dispute caused all workers on Projects 1 and 2 at Hanford to walk off the job, shutting down construction for several weeks. It was only the first of many labor walkouts and strikes which plagued the Supply System up until 1980. Stein tried continually to institute a labor stabilization agreement, but the circumstances of nuclear plant construction were against him. With almost any other construction work, delays from labor problems can be alleviated by hiring non-union laborers or by simply employing a whole new union. The complex technology of a nuclear plant and the stringent regulations impinging on it preclude such solutions to labor disputes. As one member of the WPPSS board put it, "You can't just fire all the strikers and have a whole new crew pick up the pieces from where the old one left off. There would be mass confusion." Few other industries saw labor holding management as helplessly over a barrel as did the nuclear industry of the 1970s. And WPPSS found that it was being thrust into a management position that other entities were supposed to fill.

The Supply System, for all of its ambition and self-confidence, had never intended to be drawn into the role of managing even a single nuclear plant, much less five. The founders and directors of WPPSS had meant for it to act as the *sponsor* for financing and building generating facilities. Actual management responsibilities were vested in the manager-director from the start of the Supply System, but day-to-day functions of managing projects had been, since the HGP, given over to contractors. WPPSS—the board of directors, in other words—would ideally oversee the activities of the managing firm or firms from time to time and make decisions as it saw fit. As the number of contractors multiplied and the complexity of the technical and financial aspects of the construction program skyrocketed, the WPPSS board and executive committee grew increasingly distant from the activities of the contractors. The growing gap was filled with the burgeoning "WPPSS staff"—specialized personnel hired to perform oversight tasks in all areas of the massive construction program: fiscal, legal, engineering, public relations. In short, the staff performed all the functions of a large corporation. The Supply System certainly had most of the powers of a corporation, with one important exception: It was not supposed to *be* like a corporation. The most distinctive difference between a public agency like WPPSS and an IOU, from the consumer's viewpoint, was that the public agency's rates would always be significantly lower. Yet as early as 1974, the estimated total costs for WNP-1, 2, and 3 increased by almost $1 billion from the previous year. In February of that year, Stein issued the following warning in the Supply System annual report:

> It now appears that completion of many of the thermal plants is running behind schedule. . .These delays increase plant costs for an industry already encountering high financial charges and escalating labor and equipment costs. The rising costs ultimately will be borne by the consumer in the form of higher electric rates.

Along with the nationwide competition for nuclear expertise and equipment was the search for plant sites. In the Northwest, sites for potential nuclear plants were being purchased as early as 1967, when Clark and Cowlitz county PUDs bought some land north of Vancouver, ostensibly as a site for a joint Clark/Cowlitz nuclear plant. Shortly afterward, Seattle and Snohomish PUDs bought a tiny island in Puget Sound as a likely site for a future joint nuclear effort. For a number of years during the 1970s, Pacific Power & Light had a grand plan for a complex of six nuclear power plants and four coal-fired plants to be clustered on a 5,000-acre site at Roosevelt, Washington, about 60 miles southeast of Hanford. By mid-1975, the number of planned nuclear projects in the Northwest stood at 17, with seven scheduled for completion by 1985. Prime sites for nuclear plants were hard to come by in the Pacific Northwest—thus the plans for an "energy park" at Roosevelt by PP&L.

Environmentalism was deeply entrenched in Washington, Oregon, and Montana before it became a significant political force in the 1970s (Idaho, more often than not, bucked the trend). It was ironic that Oregon, the most progressive state in the region (and perhaps the nation as well) in environmental matters, would be the location for the region's second commercial nuclear plant, Trojan, owned by Portland General Electric (70 percent) and Eugene's Water and Electric Board. The paradox was made manifest in Trojan's first years of operation, 1976 and 1977, when protest groups, notably the Trojan Decomissioning Alliance, held frequent demonstrations at the plant 30 miles northwest of Portland. Concerned Oregonians, who might have disavowed believing that a nuclear plant could be built in their state until the actual fact was undeniable, formed groups to make sure that it didn't happen again. Their immediate target was PGE's proposed Pebble Springs project, a two-unit nuclear complex planned in the eastern Oregon desert south of Arlington. The mainstay in the fight against Pebble Springs was a lawyer from the Portland suburb of Boring, Lloyd Marbet. His group, Forelaws on Board, was successful in tying up state hearings on a permit for the project for several years.

The opposition to nuclear power in Oregon reached its first crescendo in 1975, when Marbet's organization, the Coalition for Safe Power, and other local groups sponsored two state referenda: the Nuclear Safeguards Act, which would require state approval of safety devices in proposed nuclear plants; and the Nuclear Moratorium Initiative, which would institute a moratorium on the construction of such plants in Oregon until voters decided the technology was safe enough. At that time, BPA administrator Don Hodel was desperately trying to win utilities and their customers over to the nuclear plants in the Hydro-Thermal Program, which was dead in the water from a dearth of signers to the Participants' Agreements. Hodel, his patience already worn thin from two suits in the docket against him, lashed out at environmentalists in general in a July speech he made before the Portland City Club:

> Over the past few years it [the environmental movement] has fallen into the hands of a small, arrogant faction which is dedicated to bringing our society to a halt. I call this faction the prophets of shortage. Their tactics are those of confrontation rather than constructive dialogue. Their weapons are the injunction, the restraining order, and the challenge to the environmental impact statement. Their theater of operations is the courtroom, where they are always the plaintiff, never the defender. . .the anti-producers do it week in and week out, seldom winning a case but satisfied to keep progress at bay with their legal maneuvers.

Hodel admitted later in his speech, "I cannot attribute all of these [problems] to environmental pressures. Erratic federal funding, labor disputes and shortages, technical problems—all conspire to upset schedules and impede new generations from coming on line." But newspaper reports of the next day mostly ignored Hodel's qualifying statement, instead playing up his virulent criticism of the environmental movement.

Any hope of environmentalist support for Hodel's programs ended with that speech; the conservationist organizations and their allies never forgave him for his finger pointing, not even seven years later, after he had attained national office. Kai Lee, one of the Northwest's most respected thinkers on energy matters, coauthored a study in 1980 which stated:

> In light of the divisions within the electricity utility industry which have become public since 1977, Hodel's attack seems in retrospect an attempt to identify a scapegoat—one not too dangerous to criticize. If the regional power debate leads to a program superior to the utilities' hydro-thermal plans, the Northwest will have cause to thank its prophets of anticipated costs.

(Shortly after the study was published, Lee played an integral role in formulating the "superior" program.)

While the environmental movement gained strength in Oregon in 1975, it appeared to be dormant up north in Washington, except in one area of the state, where it was positively nonexistent: the Tri-Cities. It wasn't that the denizens of Kennewick, Richland, and Pasco were anti-environment—although to drive through the treeless, sun-bleached countryside surrounding the Tri-Cities one tends to wonder how a person growing up in the area could develop much of a love for nature. It is important to understand that these communities sprang out of the sagebrush and flourished on the basis of a substance which is completely artificial: plutonium. In its first phase, that of munitions producer, Hanford manufactured the deadly element as an end product; in its second phase, Hanford's primary output was (and is) nuclear energy, and plutonium thus became an undesirable by-product, an indestructible, hazardous waste that required elaborate and expensive disposal. Yet there was talk in 1975 of turning a profit on the extremely toxic stuff by making Hanford the plutonium-disposal center of the nation, wherein tons of nuclear waste from reactors around the United States would be buried beneath the desert floor. This "third phase" in Hanford's development would bring the area full circle from its role as the country's main manufacturer of plutonium to its distinction as the element's major disposer. It is not surprising that, while other nuclear research center communities such as Los Alamos, New Mexico, and Oak Ridge, Tennessee, spurned consideration as plutonium dumps, the Tri-Cities embraced the idea. After all, the area in 1975 was undergoing the biggest boom in its history, with thousands of gainfully employed new workers streaming into the towns to help build the three nuclear plants of the Supply System. They brought with them their generous salaries to increase the material wealth of the area and their staunch pro-nuclear philosophy to add to the ideological unity that made the Tri-Cities a bastion of nuclear power advocacy. The unique communal *Weltanschauung* spawned a culture of its own; businesses in Kennewick and Richland are prefaced with "atomic" this or "nuclear" that, as in "Atomic Dry Cleaners." A favorite bumper sticker around the towns was "A little nukie never hurt anybody." The atomic apotheosis approached the surreal; the Richland High School football team, calling itself "the Bombers," had a mushroom cloud emblazoned on each helmet.

It was the perfect culture for WPPSS. The Supply System and the Tri-Cities fed on each other like a happily married couple. Although WPPSS was intended to be a decentralized organization, and always had a membership which was scattered around the state, whenever one thought of WPPSS after 1970 or so, one thought of Hanford and its dependent communities. The nuclear energy route which WPPSS had chosen linked its identity with that of the Tri-Cities. In August of 1973, when the Supply System was outgrowing its headquarters in Kennewick, the director briefly discussed alternative locations for their main offices. Gordon Vickery from Seattle City Light argued that the state's largest city was the natural choice for the WPPSS central location; after all, most meetings of the board of directors and executive committee had been held there since the beginning, in 1957. Ed Fischer, Clark County PUD commissioner, wanted the headquarters moved to his hometown of Vancouver; he pointed out that it would be easier for him to stay on top of things as chairman of the executive committee if the Supply System's main office were close to where he lived. But these points were not given serious consideration, and the eventual decision of the board was to build a $2.5 million headquarters complex north of Richland, at the south edge of the Hanford reservation and within sight of the site clearing for WNP-1 and 2, and later, No. 4.

A better place to build three nuclear plants probably does not exist anywhere, for it is in their location that Plants 1, 2, and 4 were able to proceed without any significant intervention. They were being built, after all, 12 miles from the nearest residences, and these families, along with all of their neighbors, were 100 percent behind the plants. The isolated location at Hanford underscores some points that would assure that the type of on-site anti-nuclear demonstrations that were plaguing projects around the country would not take place at WNP-1, 2, and 4. First of all, the closest community that harbored any sizable nuclear protest organization was Seattle, over 200 miles away. Even if a group of protesters chose to go all the way to the Tri-Cities to demonstrate, the closest they would be able to get to the project sites would be two miles, because the sites lie that far within the restricted boundaries of the Hanford military reservation. And the demonstrators would be traveling to a hostile community in a harsh environment that is unbearably hot in the summer and bitterly cold in the winter.

Even the licensing hearings for the Hanford plants, on both state and federal levels, were virtually free of opposition, an amazing feat when compared with hearings for almost all other nuclear projects of the time. As a result, the Supply System enjoyed a reputation that, as late as 1976, was practically untarnished. Of course, this was largely due to the fact that WPPSS had little reputation to speak of, even in 1976. Most Northwesterners had never heard of WPPSS, and many of those who had did not know what it was. Even the customers of the PUDs and municipals that owned WPPSS knew little about the agency, because they dealt solely with the utilities when paying bills or making calls in regard to service. For an organization which was actively building two nuclear plants, had plans for three more, and estimated a total construction budget of $4.5 billion in 1975, the Supply System was able to keep an amazingly low profile. Outside of the Tri-Cities, WPPSS was an acronym as unfamiliar as it was unpronounceable. (Those who didn't live in that area and who knew something about the agency referred to it by its acronym, usually pronouncing it to rhyme with "cups." Tri-Cities residents and employees of WPPSS almost always called it "The Supply System.") Washington newspapers carried few stories about WPPSS until the end of 1977, with the exception of the *Tri-City Herald*, which knew that every sneeze from the Supply System could mean that the local economy would catch cold.

In general, however, most of the region took little note of what was happening in Richland, or in Seattle where the WPPSS boards continued to hold most of their meetings (which, though open to the public, were not widely advertised), or in Portland at Bonneville Power Administration headquarters, where decisions regarding the Hydro-

Thermal Power Program were linking the destinies of the region's tax-payers with WPPSS. Yet, beginning in 1976, a public awareness of the tangible effects of the Supply System construction program began to dawn on the Pacific Northwest.

On April 11, 1976, WPPSS intentionally lowered water below Priest Rapids Dam by closing the dam's floodgates, for the purpose of testing water intake mechanisms for WNP Unit No. 1. As a result, millions of salmon fry (very young, tiny fish) died from lack of sufficient water in the reach. As a result, the State Department of Fisheries filed a petition with Washington's Energy Facility Site Evaluation Committee (EFSEC). The petition asked EFSEC for suspension of certification for the operation of No. 2 (which at that time was scheduled for completion in September 1979) until WPPSS paid the Fisheries Department $1.65 million, which it estimated to be the cost of replacing the dead fish. The Supply System said it would decide how much to pay after doing its own studies of the replacement costs. Two months later, WPPSS concluded that a fair settlement would be $180,000, an offer the Fisheries Department promptly rejected. The fish kill was a black eye for the Supply System, which had prided itself for years as being a champion of conservation and effective resources management, the environmentally conscious alternative to the "wasteful" IOUs. The public relations benefits from a quick settlement with the Fisheries Department would have seemed clear, even if it meant spending a million or so; instead, WPPSS dug in, drawing attention to itself in the ensuing fight over compensation. After two years of negotiations, WPPSS finally agreed to comply to an order by EFSEC to construct ponds and other improvements to an existing fish hatchery owned by Grant County PUD near Priest Rapids, at an estimated cost of $300,000.

The Supply System's seeming shortage of largesse with respect to its ecological responsibilities even extended to its "urban impacts" on the Tri-Cities, communities that had stood by WPPSS from the beginning, rejoicing in its triumphs and sharing its pains. This harmonious relationship began to show signs of strain in early 1977, when 11 taxing districts in the Tri-Cities area formed a Construction Impact Group to study the local effects of the influx of workers directly or indirectly involved in construction of 1, 2, and 4. The group identified two primary problems: school overcrowding and traffic congestion. It also suggested that additional police be hired to deal with an expected rise in local crime. Mayor Lane Bray of Richland, who also represented the municipal utility system on the WPPSS board, was chosen as the impact group's spokesman. In May, he announced that the group was seeking $11.8 million from WPPSS in impact compensation over the 10-year construction period. The Supply System came back with a counterproposal of $1.2 million, a little over one-tenth that amount. Glen Walkley, president of the WPPSS executive committee, pointed out, "Communities here pay as much for cleanup after the Gold Cup hydroplane races as they do for cleaning up garbage for an entire year. No one's ever suggested they pay anything." Nor did anyone, it could be added, bother to remind Walkley that the effects of the annual speedboat races on the Columbia lasted for all of two days each year.

By November 16, the Construction Impact Group had adjusted its 10-year compensation request down to $9.5 million, but WPPSS wouldn't budge from its bid. Bray alleged that the agency had recently spent $8 million on a study of an 1872 North Cascades earthquake, and that "If that much could be spent on earthquake study the Supply System could spend a little more money on people." The earthquake study centered on the site which was at that time being prepared for Projects 3 and 5, near a little village in western Washington called Satsop.

Satsop sits at the confluence of the Satsop and Chehalis rivers in verdant Grays Harbor County west of Olympia. The flood plains lining the rivers are dotted with small farms, while the land that rises into high hills on each side is dark with forests of fir, spruce, and alder. About four miles east of Satsop on Highway 12 is the larger town of Elma, where logging and lumber are the mainstay businesses. All the towns in the area, in fact, are mill towns, and the people who live there are hard-working and loquacious, with a simple respect for the land, the trees, and the climate. It is a climate and a land as completely opposite to Hanford's as one could possibly imagine. It is a place where one would least expect to find a nuclear plant.

Yet Satsop is where WPPSS wanted to build two nuclear plants. It had decided to build on the site in 1973 on a heavily wooded hillside south of the little town. But even before work got under way at Satsop, the No. 2 project back at Hanford had ground to a standstill.

A four-month pipefitter's strike in 1976 crippled Project 2 long after the strike was finally ended. Progress at the plant was slowed for 10 months afterward because many of the original workers had become frustrated and taken jobs elsewhere. Each day of delay in construction added an estimated $186,000 to the project cost. Construction was so poor that WPPSS fired its general contractor, Bovee and

Crail, in January 1976. B&C sued the Supply System a month later for $24.5 million, alleging that WPPSS had breached its contract by not providing plans and specifications, issuing many vague and uncertain change orders, and failing to provide competent contract and construction administration. It also alleged "bad faith, overreaching, fraud, and other concealment" by WPPSS. WPPSS countersued for $45 million, alleging B&C failed to meet schedule dates, furnish sufficient personnel, and correct slippage in construction deadlines. The transition to a new general contractor added to the confusion: The project manager for No. 2's main electrical contractor complained that his company had been given so many out-of-date engineering drawings that it couldn't proceed. In a memo to Supply System management, he asked, "The WPPSS customers, bankers, and owners can be expected to ask, 'Is this not a wasteful use of construction dollars?' And the answer is going to be a resounding 'yes.' " In a meeting with BPA officials, Neil Strand, the WPPSS assistant director of projects, compared work at No. 2 to "going down the highway at 70 miles per hour in a defective truck while making repairs on the engine."

Managing Director J. J. Stein wrote the president of the WPPSS board in January 1977: "Until 1976, you had no effective cost controls or project estimates and the project schedule was not developed to the point where it was a satisfactory management tool." What had developed was an alarming trend in "open-ended financing." WPPSS was forbidden by state law to sign contracts that allowed companies to routinely add costs to their contracts as extraneous factors made such necessary additions in order to complete the contracted task, an arrangement known as "cost-plus" and frequently used on other nuclear construction projects. The Supply System was required to have any contract price revisions, called change orders, okayed by the board of directors. But by 1976 so many contractors were requesting change orders so often that work slowed even more while tasks with change orders were held up until the next board meeting. Therefore, WPPSS would inform a contractor to proceed with its work and the additional costs would be added to the contract later for subsequent board approval. What happened then, Stein wrote, was that "open-ended financial commitments. . .were your normal mode of operation. . . . There were no contract budgets of use to management. . . .So your unpriced notice [to contractors] to proceed was a 'blank check' payable by the Supply System from an unbalanced account."

Stein tried to institute cost-control measures in 1976, but they proved ineffective. By early 1977, according to a former member of the executive committee, Stein "looked terrible. The weight of all the problems was really taking its toll by then." The managing director was past retirement age, and it was widely agreed that he should collect his pension and step down. As the Board searched for a successor, they directed that the Supply System staff hire a company to do a study that would indicate an appropriate salary for a prospective managing director. When the conclusions of the study were revealed, the board was startled. For someone acting as top manager for a nuclear power project, the national average salary was $150,000 a year. Stein was being paid $55,000 a year when he retired in 1977. As a former member of the executive committee recalled:

> We had no idea the top managers of nuclear projects were getting paid that much in other parts of the country. . . . [Stein] mentioned [before his retirement] that he didn't think he was getting paid enough, but at the time the committee felt that his salary was adequate.

Yet the committee remained tight-fisted in considering a new manager for WPPSS. During one interview between the committee and an applicant for the job, the applicant was asked what sort of salary he expected. When his reply was over $100,000, chairman Ed Fischer informed him that that was too high, and the interview essentially ended there.

After considering several applicants from the private sector, the committee selected a man from within the Supply System: assistant director of projects Neil O. Strand. Strand was a big, affable type with an easy smile and the kind of personality that causes even sworn enemies to admit that he was "a real nice guy." He was a refreshing change from the volatile Stein, who did not seem to get along with most people. Strand was a native eastern Washingtonian who began his engineering career with General Electric at the Hanford Atomic Works in 1952, where he eventually had a hand in the design and construction of the N-reactor. In the late 1960s and early 1970s he helped GE build nuclear plants in New Jersey, Minnesota, and California. He had been working for the Supply System since 1971. Despite what the manager's salary survey showed, the board started Strand in his managing director post at $70,000 a year.

Strand began his term in the top position of WPPSS by requesting $90 million from the executive committee to help pay for construction of Nos. 4 and 5. The committee ordered a bond sale in May 1977 to cover the request. In July, the committee ordered another bond issue, this time for $230 million for No. 3. Two months later, the committee authorized yet another bond issue: $130 million, again for 4/5. Dealing with tremendous amounts of money was becoming commonplace for the executive committee, as the minutes of a typical meeting of the time seem to indicate. On June 24, 1977, for example, the committee agenda included:

| | | |
|---|---|---|
| Awarded: | $10.5 million | to Isaacson Steel for Projects 1 and 4. |
| Awarded: | $ 1.4 million | to Whiting Corporation for 1/4. |
| Awarded: | $ 2.0 million | to Northwest Construction for 1/4. |
| Awarded: | $ 324,521 | to Gould Pumps for 1/4. |
| Approved: | $ 747,000 | for a change order to Fishbach-Lord Electric for No. 2. |
| Awarded: | $ 450,000 | to Westinghouse for 3/5. |
| Awarded: | $ 103,286 | to Quigg Brothers-McDonald/GH Industrial Contractors for 3/5. |

With financing matters seemingly in hand, Strand turned his attention to Project 2, which was still suffering from a variety of ills. Strand recommended that WPPSS take over the management of the project from the AE, Burns & Roe. He was convinced that the Supply System could do a better job, in spite of the fact that it had never managed a nuclear plant construction project. The WPPSS board, which either had a great deal of faith in Strand or was truly disgusted with Burns & Roe (or both), approved of the idea. But while Strand and his staff were concentrating on taking the reins of No. 2, storm clouds were gathering over Satsop, the site of Projects 3 and 5.

The events of the wet winter of 1977-78 were not without premonition. Ever since WPPSS sent its first site scouting party in 1973, the people who lived in the Satsop area had been advising Supply System officials of the instability of the local soil under a heavy rain. The warnings continued through local site hearings for 3/5, which began in February 1974. Although no organized intervention was evident during the two years of hearings, a good deal of concern was voiced over the site location. It was pointed out that the Chehalis River, which meandered just below the hillside upon which the plants would rise, is an important medium for spawning salmon. And, many of those who testified were worried about the runoff from the proposed excavation during the area's heavy winter rainstorms. Supply System representatives assured that "redundant" erosion control measures would be used at Satsop, including an elaborate system of ditches and embankments to drain runoff appropriately. They also agreed to install a large chemical water treatment system which would "discharge" [runoff] water into the Chehalis twice as clean as Nature intended."

The site was certified by the state in October 1976, and seven months later the Nuclear Regulatory Commission issued a limited work authorization, which allowed WPPSS to begin site clearing. The WPPSS contractor, S.G. Groves Company, immediately began felling trees and moving earth across the face of the hillside. But troubles began early, almost from the first late-summer shower. Following a week of sporadic but by no means abnormal rainfall this entry was recorded for September 7 in the site log of environmental events:

> East and West ditches of plant island no longer intact. Site runoff and erosion occurred. . .down drains not placed properly; erosion control measures not keeping pace with excavation. Oil containment dike in Groves' maintenance yard broken. . . .

At this point, the normal rainy season had not even begun. Several weeks of mostly dry weather allowed the site crews to repair the damage, dig new ditches, install pumps, build check dams, and excavate two large ponds, one for settling sedimentation, the other for equalizing excessive runoff. The rain began to fall fairly steadily in late October, and within a week erosion was getting out of hand. Exactly a year before, the energy facility site evaluation committee had approved the Satsop site with a major provision being that the excavations be able to withstand 5.5 inches of rain in a 24-hour period. Less than two inches of rain was causing mudslides in October 1977. The following is a fascinating account of the events as entered in the projects' log of environmental occurrences. It outlines a story of serious underestimation of the power of natural forces, and the frantic attempts by site crews to deal with an overwhelming situation that sometimes bordered on low comedy. (A brief explanation of terms is helpful. An RR is a reservoir built to catch excessive site runoff. F-1, F-2, W-1, and P-1, P-2, etc., are pump stations, at which dammed ponds catch runoff and pumps feed the runoff into pipelines that eventually discharge water into the Chehalis River. EAR is the East Access Road. Shotrock is coarse gravel used to stabilize eroding soil. A berm is a man-made embankment.)

The problems began to escalate rapidly on October 31 with the first heavy rainfall of the season:

| Dates | Rainfall | Description |
|---|---|---|
| 10/31/77 | Heavy | Station F-1 overflowed; haybales placed below dam. F-2 began overflowing again between 530 and 0900. West Ditch received maintenance. . .Reservoir maintenance |

| Dates | Rainfall | Description |
|-------|----------|-------------|
| | | ...Reservoir RR-1 overflowed; pump installation began. New pond and dike constructed above F-1...Reservoir RR-2 overflowed. Original P-1 dike eroded. Slopes and ditches...on EAR needed extensive work.... |
| 11/01/77 | Heavy with severe winds | F-1 and F-2 overflowed. Pipelines at P-2, P-3, and W-1 ruptured by falling trees. Reservoirs RR-1 and RR-2 overflowed; pump installation continued....Slopes in upper Stein Creek basin began sliding. P-4 overflowed. Slope...on west side of EAR slid... |
| 11/03/77 | Little | F-1 remained silted in. F-2 overflowed intermittantly. Major slide occurred in upper Stein Creek basin; slide material completely filled W-1 pond....Additional shotrock placed in ditch on EAR.... |
| 11/04/77 | Little | F-2 overflowed approximately 35-50 gpm [gallons per minute]. Slight overflow (30-50 gpm) from equalization pond to settling pond....W-1 inoperable; overflowed 200-300 gpm. Ditches along EAR...were sandbagged....Shotrock placed in ditches from Stations 38 to 49....Sandbags installed on upper berm.... |
| 11/07/77 | Little | Chemical treatment system under repair; no water bypassed to Chehalis River. Approximately four feet of freeboard [space between water level and rim of containment dike] in equalization pond....Slide occurred along EAR....Oil film observed in West Ditch....Laborers began mucking out W-1.... |
| 11/08/77 | Some | W-1 remained inoperable and overflowing; safety factor prevented repair work. Discussions concerning feed rate for chemical treatment began between the Supply System and Ebasco.... |
| 11/10/77 | Little | ...Settling pond began overflowing through cracks in discharge line. Repair of discharge line begun. F-2, RR-2, and W-1 overflowed. ...Maintenance continued in West Ditch. |

| Dates | Rainfall | Description |
|---|---|---|
| | | F-1 dike heightened; silt reservoir under construction upstream of F-1. Small slide occurred at EAR Station 47 + 50. |
| 11/11/77 | Some | Repair work continued on settling pond discharge line. Very little freeboard in equalization pond....W-1 continued to overflow. Slide occurred on EAR Stations 47 + 50 to 48 + 50. |
| 11/13/77 | Heavy | All stop logs [for shoring up containment dikes] installed in equalization pond; water rose and began overflowing stop logs. More sandbags installed at emergency overflow. West Ditch nearly overtopped at intersection with East Ditch. Repair work continued on settling pond discharge line. |
| 11/14/77 | Rained | Water released through emergency overflow of equalization pond at 0215 hours at about 23 cubic feet per second. Repair work continued on settling pond discharge line.... |
| 11/15/77 | Some | ...Water continued to discharge through equalization pond emergency spillway. East Ditch received maintenance; east berm 100 yards upstream of P-1 pipeline discharge slid away. Slides occurred on EAR Stations 43, 47 + 50 and 112....W-1 continued to overflow. |

By this time the entire site had become such a massive quagmire that even some of the earth-moving equipment was inoperable. Emergency overflows had to bypass the chemical water treatment system, which was overloaded anyway. On November 17 Strand issued a stop-work order for Projects 3 and 5, in order for the erosion control system to be brought into some level of effectiveness. An emergency operations center was established at the 3/5 field office, and the management of flood control was put on a "priority basis" around the clock, seven days a week. Of the 400 personnel involved in site work, most were non-manual workers; therefore all but about 150 were sent on temporary leaves with pay until the situation could be brought under control. A four-day break in the weather gave the work crews a chance to do repairs to severely damaged dikes, ponds, and pumps. But it was only the calm before the storm—a storm that would turn out to be the worst rainstorm to hit the area in 20 years. The rains began on November 22; they would continue to fall without ceasing for the next eight weeks.

| Dates | Rainfall | Description |
|---|---|---|
| 11/22/77 | Little | Continued desilting P-1 constructing road by settling pond, and excavating unstable material in upper Stein Creek basin. Severe erosion observed between EAR stations 48 and 49. Repair work continued on settling good discharge line. Construction of reservoir dikes above F-1 and F-2 continued. Construction of all-weather road to F-2 began.... |
| 11/23/77-11/24/77 | Heavy | Wind action caused bypassing of water down equalization pond emergency overflow. F-2 pumping discontinued because of equalization pond overflow. Construction of interceptor ditch parallel and east of West Ditch begun. Slides noted in Elizabeth and Hyatt creeks area.... |
| 11/25/77-11/27/77 | Heavy | W-1, P-4, F-1, and F-2 overflowed. Water continued to bypass down equalization pond emergency overflow....Discharging began through the repaired settling pond discharge line on November 25, at about 2500 hrs, with a flow of about 5000 gpm; on November 26, at 1500 hrs, the flow was 7300 gpm; and on November 26, at 1800 hrs, it was 9500 gpm. Excavation of unstable material in upper Stein Creek continued. West Ditch was lined with plastic. |
| 11/28/77-11/29/77 | Rained | ....Haybale check dams at the mouth of Stein Creek were noted as undercut or nonfunctional. Excavation of unstable material in upper Stein Creek basin continued. W-1 and P-4 overflowed. P-1 was relocated on a new dike about 200 yards downstream of the old dike. Repair work started on breaks in the emergency overflow line from the equalization pond. Oil sheens were observed in East and West ditches. Groves' maintenance yard was noted as needing extensive cleanup as required by |

| Dates | Rainfall | Description |
| --- | --- | --- |
| | | the Oil Spill Prevention and Countermeasure Plan. Began installation of permanent plant storm drain pipe. Repairs needed on oil skimmer boards in settling ponds. RR-1 silted in. |
| 11/30/77 | Rained | Excavation in upper Stein Creek basin, steel pipeline construction from P-4 to P-3, and construction of silt dike above F-2 continued. P-4 was desilted. Slides were observed on EAR Stations 48 through 49 + 50 and 66.... |

On the first day of December, the heavens opened on the hapless Satsop project site.

| Dates | Rainfall | Description |
| --- | --- | --- |
| 12/01/77- 12/02/77 | Extremely heavy (5.21 in in 24 hrs) | Pump stations P-1, P-2, P-3, P-4, W-1, F-2, F-1, RR-1 and RR-2 overflowed. Desilting operations stopped at P-4 for safety reasons. P-3 dike was leaking. W-1 dike overtopped and began eroding. RR-1 waters were pumped directly to the Chehalis River. Three slides occurred along the Union Pacific Railroad between RR-2 and the settling pond discharge line. Plastic was installed on outside wall of East Ditch in warehouse fill area. West Ditch near equalization pond was overtopping because of undersized culverts....Erosion and slides observed on EAR between Stations 66 and 67. Oil boom missing at Station P-4.... Keyes Road slid away about 300 yards north of security check point (road impassible). Water washed over low portions of Workman Creek Road near security check point. Chehalis River at flood stage. |
| 12/03/77- 12/04/77 | Some | W-1, P-3, P-4, F-1, and F-2 were out of commission. Station RR-1 continued to pump to the Chehalis River. RR-2 overflowed. Repair work was done on interceptor and West ditches....The Chehalis River remained at flood stage. |

| Dates | Rainfall | Description |
|-------|----------|-------------|
| 12/05/77-<br>12/06/77 | Heavy | F-1, F-2, P-4 and W-1 overflowed....Serious erosion was observed on EAR slopes. The Chehalis River remained at flood stage. |

On December 9, a dam on Stein Creek was breached, huge faults opened up along the perimeter of the excavated area, and a large portion of the site began to slide into the Chehalis River. For the next two days, the Satsop project was in violation of state and federal environmental laws, but the site manager was more concerned with merely keeping the whole operation from being washed away. Tons of shotrock were hauled in around the clock in attempts to stabilize the shifting soil. Fifteen thousand square feet of plastic were spread out over critically eroding areas. The efforts were hampered by limited site access due to the mudslide that carried part of Keyes Road down the hillside.

While Satsop was being turned into a sea of mud, the WPPSS board and executive committee were briefed by Supply System staff. No discussion ever followed these meeting briefings—not a single question about the flooding, what was being done about it, and how much it would cost. When dry weather returned at last in the spring of 1978, a massive earth-moving operation was ordered, which leveled an area around the plants to twice the size of the original site. In August 1978 the WPPSS board approved $51 million in cost overruns for site preparation at 3/5. Long before then, the environmental movement had finally caught up with the Supply System.

# 8

# OUT OF CONTROL

By early 1977, environmentalist groups in Washington state were rousing themselves from the somnambulant stance they had taken with regard to the WPPSS construction program. The stimulant was a study begun in the spring of 1975 at the behest of the Seattle city council. Seattle had been asked by BPA and the Public Power Council to participate in WNP-4 and 5 by purchasing a 10 percent share of each. But the study, entitled *Energy 1990* and completed in February 1976, recommended instead that the city invest in a moderately aggressive energy conservation program, a conclusion which unleashed a storm of controversy. In July, the city council adopted the recommendation of *Energy 1990* by a six-to-three vote, opting against participation in 4/5. City Light supervisor Gordon Vickery proposed that SCL halve the original request of a 10 percent share, which would put Seattle's ownership in each project at 5 percent. The city council rejected the proposal. It also rejected Vickery's recommendation of a 1 percent share as a sign of at least token support for Phase II of the Hydro-Thermal Power Program.

*Energy 1990* gave environmentalists a political boost of confidence, and they began to express criticism of the WPPSS program. Their most frequent complaint was that WPPSS was not listening to its customers, that it was no longer accountable to the desires of the ratepayers. Martin Baker, former executive director of the Washington Environmental Council, commented in early 1977:

Unknown to most people, WPPSS is creating the electricity future of the
state of Washington—without the participation of the people who have
to pay the bills. The unfortunate thing is that they're so efficient and slick
in what they do they haven't thought seriously about alternatives, and
therefore are failing to become responsible leaders not only in the production of power, but in the conservation of resources.

Yet, the public image of the Supply System was becoming one in
which few would find reason to believe that it could be "efficient and
slick" in anything. In January of 1978, information on the problems
at Satsop began trickling out of WPPSS board meetings, which were
open to the press and public but sparsely attended by those groups.
However, in May the *Bellingham Herald* did a special report on relations between WPPSS and the Energy Facility Siting Evaluation Council, in which members of EFSEC voiced some astonishing feelings
about the Supply System's finances and general attitude. "Some of the
members," said the *Herald*, "have labeled the system pushy, unrespon-
sive, and a less than cooperative public agency." Nick Lewis, chairman
of EFSEC, said he was concerned because WPPSS was "borrowing
money right and left. . .and yet it fights over compensation for the
Columbia River fish kill [in April 1976]." The erosion problems at
Satsop caused a great deal of concern at EFSEC, said Lewis: "I felt
several times we had their attention and the erosion problem would
be solved. But then there was the dawning realization that it wasn't
enough to get their attention; we had to get on their bloody backs!"

Lewis noted, "We get a lot more cooperation out of the private
utilities than we get out of the Supply System." He and other EFSEC
members agreed that Puget Sound Power & Light was much more cooperative in hearings for its proposed nuclear plants in the Skagit Valley. "Puget did a significantly better job, essentially on a volunteer
basis [than did WPPSS]," said Malachy Murphy, who served as state
counsel for the environment on nuclear siting cases. Fred Clagett, who
had been a WPPSS board member representing Richland in 1968 and
1969, was on the other side of the fence in 1978 as a member of EFSEC.
He told the *Herald* of his frustration at meetings between WPPSS and
EFSEC:

> I was always left with the uneasy feeling that rather than do something
> in a way to ensure they met requirements, WPPSS would shade it so close
> we would always have an argument on our hands about whether or not
> they met the standards. At times during my experience on the council I
> felt WPPSS was less than forthright. If we did not ask the right questions,
> we did not get the right anwers. . . .

The *Herald* allowed the Supply System equal space in its report. John Goldsbury, Benton County PUD commissioner and president of the WPPSS board, responded to environmentalist concerns about accountability by saying, "All board members are elected people—how could [the board] be more responsive?" He said few members of the public attend WPPSS meetings. "I construe that as saying the people think we are doing a good job. When we start getting pressure from the people, that is when we're not doing a good job." Strand was asked if he thought that Supply System haggling over compensation for the 1976 fish kill had given WPPSS "undesirable publicity." He agreed that it had, and added:

> However, the price to capitulate to offers we did not think were fair would not have been in the best interests of the ratepayers. . . .I would be derelict in my duty if I did not take the position of ratepayers. We have to strike the best balanced interest for ratepayers. There has to be some give and take. Perhaps our exploring for the best solution to problems is interpreted by some as being disagreeable.

Obviously, Strand firmly believed that it was the Supply System, not EFSEC, which best represented the public interest.

At least one group did not share Strand's views. The Crabshell Alliance was the first organization formed specifically to oppose the WPPSS construction program (later they also protested the basing of Trident nuclear submarines in Puget Sound). On June 24 and 25, 1978, about 200 adherents of the Crabshell Alliance and interested onlookers gathered at the Satsop site for what they called a "reclamation." The demonstration was very amicable, even when the demonstrators attempted to occupy the WPPSS property; they were met at the perimeter by a cordon of security guards, who merely toted the trespassers to waiting buses, which then hauled them away. One hundred and fifty-six people were arrested, but if not for that the whole affair could have been a bucolic little folk festival on the primeval hillside.

The Crabshell Alliance did not limit itself to mere displays of dissent; in July the Alliance filed suit in Grays Harbor County against WPPSS, challenging the legality of its construction program. Crabshell spokesman George DuVall attended a meeting of the WPPSS board to outline the position of his group. Board member Vickery then warned the board that "this could affect these plants to the tune of millions of dollars." Strand agreed, and told DuVall that if the suit affected bond rates in future sales, WPPSS would move to recover the resulting millions of dollars in costs from the Alliance. After the meeting, DuVall remarked that Strand's remarks were "a bit humorous," since the Alliance's "current assets are closer to tens of dollars than to tens of millions."

A month later, the Seattle *Post-Intelligencer* reported that the WPPSS board approved $51 million in cost overruns for erosion control at Satsop. WPPSS had negotiated a $21.6 million site-preparation contract two years before, but the disastrous effects of the 1977-78 winter had increased costs to $72.9 million by May. Jim Duree, an attorney from Westport on the coast west of Satsop, angrily criticized the Supply System's project:

> They had picked a very poor site. It shows that their [initial site] investigation was shoddy at best. And you and I, as utility customers, will end up footing the bill. In any city, county, or state government, a 231 percent cost overrun would bring cries for recall of officials, investigations, and maybe even a convening of a grand jury.

Frank McGelwee, assistant director for projects, admitted that WPPSS had "learned some lessons" about the soil at 3/5, discovering among other things that it was 40 percent moisture and 40 percent fine and "very difficult to work with. . .when you're trying to build an embankment. . . .What was not anticipated was the slide we would have in the upper reaches of Stein Creek. . . .We had not anticipated pumping stations, sediment ponds, and check dams."

A WPPSS publicity film made later and shown to thousands who visited the Supply System's 3/5 Visitor's Center at Elma, concluded:

> The erosion control program at the Satsop Power Plants is a good example of how the Washington Public Power Supply System uses creative engineering to ensure that its projects are constructed and operated with minimum environmental impact.

The film cost $150,000 to make. The total cost of the erosion crisis at Satsop, including cost overruns and the added expenses of delays and accrued interest, was over $160 million.

While the pressure was building on WPPSS from environmentalist groups, a much more significant agency was also taking a confrontational posture in its relationship with the Supply System: the Bonneville Power Administration. The alliance between the two major public-power entities of the region began to deteriorate on September 14, 1977. On that date, the U.S. Interior Department's Office of Audit and Investigation released a report on BPA responsibility for WPPSS management of construction of the net-billed plants. The study contended that Bonneville had not fulfilled its "inherent responsibility" to monitor WNP-1, 2, and 4, attributing much of the oversight problem to the "lack of an effective enforcement mechanism" and to the fact that BPA "has never formally defined its oversight role or a plan for accomplishing it." It cited disagreements between BPA and WPPSS over BPA's role in decision making. "In essence, WPPSS neither feels compelled nor obligated to respond to [BPA's] comments and on many issues, [BPA's] right to comment is challenged." On the other hand, said the report, WPPSS officials have argued that BPA's "oversight efforts are unguided, haphazard, and ineffective."

The report was circulated only to top officials at BPA and WPPSS, and to selected members of Congress. Neither Hodel nor Strand ever commented on it. Indeed, each was occupied with accounting for more than enough problems as it was. At Bonneville, the Hodel Administration was drawing to an ignominious close as the BPA chief prepared to move on to a new post at the Interior Department. The Hydro-Thermal Power Program was in a shambles. Bonneville's budget deficits were at record highs, despite a substantial increase in wholesale rates.

Hodel's successor was Sterling Munro, a long-time protégé of Scoop Jackson. When a copy of Interior's study of the BPA-WPPSS relationship was leaked to the press by a source within the Northwest's congressional delegation, Munro said that he had no quarrel with the report's conclusions and that he would seek outside advice concerning his oversight role with respect to the Supply System: "We are taking steps preparatory to bringing in some outside help to assist us in this regard. I think we need an independent look by folks who have experience in the construction of nuclear plants and [who are able] to advise us how to make our role more effective in helping WPPSS."

Munro's words stirred resentment in Richland; Supply System officials mumbled in private that they didn't need the kind of help the new administrator was talking about. In July, 1978, BPA hired Theodore Barry & Associates of Los Angeles to do a $190,700 management study of WPPSS. Strand and his staff were angry because they were not consulted about selection of the management-auditing group. Munro made it clear that the kid gloves with which Hodel handled the Supply System were off, and he and his staff became increasingly bold in criticizing WPPSS. In November of 1978, Tom Wagenhoffer, BPA's chief liaison with WPPSS, reported to a WPPSS board meeting that BPA had seen a growth pattern in employment rolls "that is alarming to us in total numbers." He hinted that WPPSS was top-heavy with unnecessary employees in top management positions, and asked the Supply System to begin a study of employment rolls. Some of the board members, particularly Glenn Walkley and board president John Goldsbury, protested Bonneville's directives. They considered them intrusions in the affairs of the Supply System. But Munro insisted that he had a right to know how federal finances backing WNP-1, 2, and 3 were being utilized.

As the time for the unveiling of the Barry management report grew near, the WPPSS executive committee attempted to hold a closed meeting to discuss the implications of the report. But a Superior Court judge issued a restraining order against the meeting, ruling that the meeting's topic was in the public interest and therefore should be open to public participation in the WPPSS boardroom. The committee cancelled the meeting.

The Barry report was presented before the WPPSS board, members of BPA, Munro, and over 200 interested persons on January 5, 1979, in the Seattle Center's Olympic Auditorium. It revealed that the WPPSS plants would cost $1.1 billion more than the Supply System's latest estimate, for a total of $8.7 billion. It concluded that there was a critical need for improvement in WPPSS management of projects, and suggested that BPA take a stronger overseer role in Supply System business. "Perhaps the most serious weakness," said the report, "is the lack of effective checks and balances upon the Supply System's operations, both from external and internal sources."

Bill Hulbert of the WPPSS executive committee hailed the Barry report as a "superior work," backed further Bonneville oversight of the projects, and blasted the WPPSS staff for not providing the board with the kind of information contained in the report. "That tells how bad things are," he noted, "but I don't get this from staff briefings of the board. I always hear how rosy it is from our staff."

Walkley and Goldsbury took the opposite point of view. Goldsbury said he had formed a committee to check into Barry's background and find out how well the group did on previous jobs. Walkley tried to turn the criticism to Bonneville. He said: "I was not enthused with this report. It missed the point. You can't tell me we put these things through without BPA's approval." He stated that the cost of the Barry report had increased from its original estimate, noting that "it will cost the ratepayers a million dollars." Munro denied this, putting the final cost of the report at $240,000. He said that he planned to begin attending Supply System board meetings whenever possible.

By April, the relationship between BPA and WPPSS had deteriorated to the point at which cooperative efforts were impossible. In a letter to top BPA officials, Munro cited numerous instances in which his aides had been excluded from WPPSS board meetings, denied information, and supplied with incomplete data by the Supply System. BPA requests to sit in on WPPSS staff meetings had been denied, Munro's letter said. It also noted that the Barry report had suggested that a written agreement be signed between BPA and WPPSS over BPA's oversight role, but that Munro's attempts to get the WPPSS board to sign such an agreement had been rebuffed. Asked by a newspaper reporter to comment on the letter, Goldsbury said that the letter had been discussed among WPPSS officials, but added that he did not know if the situation "requires a response." He then opined that Munro's criticisms were "politically motivated," and stated that he had it on good authority that the BPA administrator was interested in succeeding Warren Magnuson in the U.S. Senate. A spokesman for BPA responded to Goldsbury's comments, calling them "total nonsense."

Bonneville's frustrations over WPPSS belligerence forced the federal agency to incite public pressure against the Supply System. BPA began to leak internal documents to the press which revealed the true extent of mismanagement and confusion at the WNP projects. Among the leaked material was a memo written by an official of Burns & Roe, the AE for No. 2, to the head of the project's quality assurance division. The memo read:

> We have concluded beyond a reasonable doubt that the extensive cracking and weld defects discovered at WNP-2 resulted from inadequate weld procedures. . .and the lack of inspection during welding to assure that the requirements were, in fact, being met.
>
> To be more concise, we had what amounts to a total breakdown in quality control in this area.

A memo from a metallurgist who had warned of the unsuitability of weld joints at No. 2 said: "I got no response. .except I was told that WPPSS wanted the contractor to flounder. . . ." The metallurgist said that his whistle-blowing attempts put him at odds with his supervisors, adding that he was subjected to an "abnormal amount of job harassment, unprofessional conduct, and actions to delay my productivity." Another memo from a small contractor's project manager described the lack of effective written procedures at No. 2 as "madness." He predicted that his firm, Livermore Rebar Incorporated, would go bankrupt if improvements were not made. Five months later, the company went broke.

Toward the end of 1979, such horror stories became almost regular fare in local newspapers, particularly the Seattle *Post-Intelligencer*, which frequently called for a concerted effort from government leaders to get WPPSS under control. But the problems of the Supply System had become so complex that any plan for resolving them carried a high risk of failure; therefore, politicians shied away from taking a leadership role in dealing with WPPSS.

But in December 1979, BPA increased its rates a whopping 107 percent, and the resulting public outcry brought the region's leaders to a realization that something had to be done. Behind the scenes, WPPSS board members were receiving quiet pressure from aides to the governor, congressmen, and public power leaders of the state of Washington. The board members had seen the pressure coming months before, and they reluctantly acknowledged that there was no doubt about the imperative now required of them. By the end of the year, the message was coming in from every corner of the region: Get rid of Strand.

The beginning of 1980 brought a determined sort of relief to Supply System headquarters. The staff was glad to see 1979 go; it had been a tough year.

But the years to come would be much, much worse.

# 9

# THE DREAM CRUMBLES

On February 8, 1980, the WPPSS executive committee fired Neil Strand as managing director, and events moved rapidly toward their disastrous denouement.

The new managing director, Robert L. Ferguson, was named in June. A physicist with over 25 years of experience in the nuclear industry, Bob Ferguson had a reputation as a no-nonsense manager. He served from 1973 to 1978 as director of the fast-flux test reactor at Hanford, and afterward he was appointed deputy assistant secretary for the Department of Energy's nuclear programs. The Supply System's board of directors, so reluctant to pay the price of an experienced program director in 1977, willingly gave Ferguson a salary of $125,000 a year. From his first day on the job in August, Ferguson made it clear that he believed in a radical approach to turn the construction program around. Within months he had acheived a major shake-up of top WPPSS management, replacing virtually the entire senior staff. He assigned new project directors for each of the units. He hired Bechtel Corporation to replace the Supply System as construction manager on Projects 1, 2, and 4, and instituted a new contracting system which paid incentives for work completed on schedule. He was able to eventually work out labor arrangements which so strongly discouraged strikes and walkouts that only one instance of significant labor trouble left a blot on his term.

But the reforms came too late. Just before Ferguson took over, WPPSS adopted a 1981 construction budget which showed costs skyrocketing to nearly $16 billion, an increase of 50 percent, or more than $5 billion, over the previous year's estimates. The board was even more disheartened when staff analysts informed them that the estimate was so conservative that there was only about a one-in-five chance it would be accurate. Even if the estimate proved correct, it would require WPPSS to borrow an average of more than $1 billion a year for the next five years.

Borrowing such staggering amounts was becoming more and more problematical for the Supply System. Until 1979, the vast majority of buyers of WPPSS bonds were institutions—banks, insurance companies, and corporate portfolios. But by the late 1970s, institutional interest in new WPPSS bond releases had cooled. For one thing, the whispered fears of a Supply System saturation of the market that had been making the rounds on Wall Street since 1975 were beginning to come true. In 1978, 20 percent of all gas and electric revenue bonds sold were WPPSS bonds; in 1979, the WPPSS portion of that market was 21 percent; in 1980, 23 percent. The heavy volume was having an effect on WPPSS interest rates; in the year from December 1979 to December 1980, WPPSS costs to borrow increased by more than 350 basis points, adding hundreds of millions to the agency's long-term debt. Yet the two major bond rating agencies consistently awarded all Supply System bonds their highest ratings: Moody's rated Projects 1, 2, and 3 Aaa, and Projects 4 and 5 A1; Standard & Poor's similarly gave Projects 1, 2, and 3 its AAA rating, and Projects 4 and 5 an A-plus. The ratings were taken less and less seriously, however.

In his documentary article, "WPPSS: From Dream to Default," Wall Street analyst Howard Gleckman notes, "By the end of 1978, it was an open secret on Wall Street that Project 1, 2, and 3 bonds were no longer trading like AAA investments." Gleckman says that the sheer enormity of WPPSS bond issues was at least as important as declining investor confidence for the dampening of interest in WNP bonds.

> Property and casualty insurance companies, long a mainstay in the municipal market, were gradually withdrawing as their needs for tax-exempt income declined. In addition, many institutional investors, who were limited in the amount of a single issuer's bonds they could hold at one time, were beginning to reach those ceilings. While the yields on WPPSS bonds were very attractive, the risk was beginning to bother portfolio managers.
>
> In September 1979, in the midst of an investor tour, a representative of a large mutual fund complex walked out of a session with WPPSS

officials, found a pay phone, and called his main office. His message: "Sell everything."

The representative says today that the tour convinced him that WPPSS simply could not handle construction of five nuclear projects at one time. The "icing on the cake" came, he says, when a welder at one of the projects told him the work was so lucrative because "we do the job wrong on regular time so we can do it right on overtime."

By late 1980, WPPSS was selling bonds every 45 days, at $200 million a shot. Payments simply for interest on the debt from direct construction costs by that time were responsible for over half of the borrowings. A feeling of quiet desperation began to sink in at the headquarters in Richland and in the boardrooms in Seattle. A member of the WPPSS staff described it:

> After a bond sale, you'd think, "Okay, that should take care of our needs for the rest of this quarter." A month and a half later, we'd have to have another, bigger bond sale, and then you'd think again, "All right, that should easily be enough for a while." But then we'd have to come up with some more money even sooner than last time. You kept wishing that things would somehow get better, but they kept getting worse.

Years later, Supply System officials and board members admitted to having the same hopes during that time, though none of them could provide a substantive basis for those hopes. A former member of the board said, "What else could you do but hope? Every time someone would come up with a possible solution to the problems, Bonneville, or one of the participants, or Congress would come back and say 'That's unacceptable.'"

One of these ideas was a moratorium on construction of Projects 4 and 5. The staff began quietly studying the option in Febuary 1981, but on April 13 it concluded, "Cost increases due to delays are so significant compared to potential interest cost savings that intentional delay should be completely ruled out." But a few weeks later, a separate staff task force gave Ferguson some figures that foresaw cost increases that no one had even dreamed of. Ferguson had commissioned the group shortly after he became managing director to do what he called a "bottoms-up review" of WPPSS budgets and construction schedules. The work group would do what had never been done before: evaluate every contract for every project and realistically predict how much more time and money would be needed to complete them. After eight months of number-crunching, the group presented its findings to the WPPSS boss. Ferguson was incredulous; he immediately told the group to go back and check the figures, then recheck them. This was done, but the conclusions were basically the same. On May 29, 1981, Ferguson took the review to a meeting of the WPPSS board at its offices at Sea-Tac Airport outside Seattle. He told the directors that the five nuclear projects, which originally had been estimated to cost $4 billion, were going to cost over $24 billion.

The board members were stunned, but Ferguson wasn't finished: WPPSS would have to borrow more than $3 billion over the next year to keep the five units on schedule, a feat that was probably impossible, he said. He recommended a one-year moratorium on 4 and 5, which were responsible for half of the total costs. During the moratorium, he said, WPPSS would concentrate on expediting construction of WNP-1, 2, and 3, and in the meantime search for solutions to the 4/5 financing problem.

Ferguson's announcement had far-reaching repercussions. On Wall Street, Eileen Austen of the investment firm Drexel Burnham Lambert Incorporated became the first securities analyst to predict that Projects 4 and 5 would be cancelled. Her report and her subsequent analyses were widely read and gained credibility as their predictions were borne out. The rating agencies, optimistic to a fault, found the WPPSS $10 billion budget jump a bit hard to swallow. Standard & Poor's downgraded 4/5 from A-plus to A—still investment-grade—while Moody's dropped its rating from A1 to Baa1. The red flags came too late for investors in 4/5, many of whom were by this time "little people." When institutions had slowed purchases of WNP bonds in 1979, securities firms and brokers turned to retail buyers—individuals, small companies, and bondholder "clubs"—to take up the slack. Tens of thousands of bonds, no one is sure precisely how many, were sold to individuals or families who saw the securities as "nest eggs." Most of the $200 million in bonds sold by WPPSS in its last 4/5 issue in March 1981 probably went to retail buyers. Many of these would swear in later years that they were not informed of the many risks inherent in those bonds, although it is more than likely that the brokers who sold them were aware of the risks.

Closer to home, an amazing grass-roots movement was rising throughout the Northwest in reaction to the WPPSS costs which were spreading through the BPA rate system like a cancer. The movement was unprecedented in its spontaneity, cutting across the whole range of ideological and economic groups. With no traditional power bases or political conduits to work from or through, the movement nonetheless captured the attention and apparently the sympathy of most of the region's population. It was called the "ratepayer movement." Like the Crabshell Alliance of 1977, the ratepayers' groups of 1980-82 opposed the Supply System's nuclear construction program, but for a different reason. The Alliance had protested the program for environmental and health reasons; the new ratepayer resisters' cause was almost purely economic. As Gleckman would later write, "The conventional wisdom had been that the Northwest's base costs were so low that ratepayers would accept major cost increases without complaint. . . .The ratepayer movement showed the theory's political weakness." The people of the Northwest, generally a pragmatic and frugal lot, were simply fed up with what one group said was "WPPSS's arrogant history of throwing good money after bad." WPPSS attempts to assuage ratepayer fury by pointing out the plants' energy needs were rebuffed. As one angry letter to the editor of the Seattle *Post-Intelligencer* said:

> WPPSS says that it is building five nuclear plants so that there will be enough electricity for the next generation. That's like a man building five houses at once because he knows that the average person will live in five different places during his lifetime.

The ratepayer rebellion of the early 1980s at last made WPPSS a household acronym around the region. Most people gave it the derisive pronunciation "whoops," and made the agency an object of ridicule and the butt of innumerable jokes told with bitter laughter. The Supply System was seen by the activists as a faceless, unfeeling bureaucracy, isolated from the regional mainstream in its pro-nuclear desert fortress in the Tri-Cities. The WPPSS directors were criticized as being secretive and unrepresentative of ratepayers' interests. A common blast was that the directors were incompetent, knowledgeable in running their muffler shops, hardware stores, and apple orchards, but completely inept at building nuclear plants.

In early July 1981, a group called Don't Bankrupt Washington filed 188,000 signatures in Olympia, more than enough to place an initiative requiring voter approval for all major power project financings on the November ballot. Called Initiative 394, it was overwhelmingly approved by state voters, and any future bond sales by WPPSS were in jeopardy. Meanwhile, Ferguson was trying to put together a "mothballing" plan for 4/5 which he hoped would finance a construction delay long enough for BPA to decide to sponsor a federal program that would pump government dollars into the projects. But Bonneville, under new administrator Peter Johnson, was hinting broadly that it did not want the two plants. An internal estimate of power demands by BPA showed that 4 and 5 would not be needed for at least 10 years.

On December 26, ratepayers in Springfield, Oregon, sued the Springfield Utility Board to prohibit it from paying its share of the 4/5 debt. The suit was the first filed by ratepayers in connection to the WPPSS situation. There would be many more.

On January 5, 1982, Clark County PUD, reflecting the view of its commissioner Ed Fischer, said it would refuse to help finance the construction halt on 4/5. The next day, Moody's suspended its rating on the two units, and the Washington legislature released the results of an independent review of the plants which it had commissioned a year before; the conclusion was that it would be impossible to finance continued construction. Ferguson had no choice but to recommend the cancellation of the two projects. On January 22, the board voted to terminate WNP-4 and 5.

With I-394 due to take effect later in the year, WPPSS was unsure of future financing capabilities. It followed the abandonment of 4/5 with a record bond issue of $850 million. Investors, including many individuals, bought up the WNP-1, 2, and 3 bonds quickly, because the very high net interest cost of 14.79 percent made them extremely attractive, despite the risks involved. Ratepayer groups, furious that the Supply System was spending money more breathtakingly than ever, organized marches in locations across the region to vent their anger. PUD commissioners who attempted to explain their actions before ratepayer rallies were often booed or shouted down. Recall efforts to oust commissioners were begun in several districts.

In April, with new rate increases looming on the horizon, Bonneville's Johnson recommended that WPPSS halt construction on Project 1 for up to five years. The people of the Tri-Cities, who had watched over 2,000 workers being laid off from No. 1's cancelled twin No. 4, did not stand by for Hanford's latest setback. On the day that the WPPSS board was to make its decision on Johnson's recommendation, over 6,000 people, many of them workers from the nearby No. 2 project as well as those from WNP-1 itself, rallied in front of Supply System headquarters in the largest "pro-nuke" rally in history. The WPPSS board, however, had little choice; as the financial backer for 100 percent of No. 1, BPA had the final say in the future of that particular project. The days when WPPSS could stand up to Bonneville were over forever.

On April 26, a group of 12 rural electric cooperatives asked a Washington state court to rule on whether they were obligated to repay their share of the debt for 4/5. They were only the first of many utilities that dared to think the unthinkable: reneging on the Participants' Agreements.

WPPSS made its last bond sale on May 17: $680 million for Projects 2 and 3. At the time, most observers believed that the Supply System would somehow be able to continue borrowing in the near future; subsequent events wiped out that possibility.

On May 18, the bondholders joined the legal battle over the 4/5 debt. Alarmed by the trend of utilities trying to back out of their obligations, owners of 4/5 bonds requested Chemical Bank of New York, trustee for the bond fund, to file suit in King County Superior Court in Seattle against the 88 participants. The Chemical Bank suit thus became part of a flood of litigation involving the WPPSS projects which collectively became known as the "Lawyers' Relief Act of 1982."

In June, the Pacific Northwest Utilities Conference Committee released its latest 20-year load forecast. The forecast indicated that expectations of demand for electricity were down sharply from the previous year's forecast. The output from Projects 4 and 5, which had been crucial to the region's well-being according to PNUCC's reports only five years before, were not included in the 1982 forecast, yet the forecast showed that they would not have been needed for at least 10 years.

That same month, Portland General Electric finally abandoned plans for the Pebble Springs nuclear plants, after an investment of eight years' work and over $500 million. Puget Sound Power & Light and Pacific Power & Light, which owned shares of Pebble Springs, agreed to absorb their portions of the "dry hole," acknowledging that the output from the plants would not be needed for many years. Pebble Springs 1 and 2 never got off the drawing boards; all that remains today of the project are the faint outlines of a ditch in the Oregon desert, at the site proposed for the state's last planned nuclear plants.

The scrapping of Pebble Springs left PSP&L as the last agency besides WPPSS still planning a nuclear project in the region. Skagit 1 and 2, which PSP&L had originally planned to build in the Skagit Valley 100 miles northeast of Seattle, were still being included in regional plans as late as 1983, even though the plants were still in the preconstruction phase. Due to strong environmental opposition in the Skagit Valley, the project's planned site had been moved to Hanford.

Meanwhile, the ratepayers of the Northwest, having vented their frustration through various demonstrations of their discontent, began a call for political leadership to lead the region out of its morass. But government and utility leaders complained that policy making had been taken out of their hands and put into those of the attorneys and judges involved in the growing number of court cases over the future of WPPSS. There was one unique entity that offered a glimmer of hope to the region: the Regional Power Planning Council. The Council had been formed as part of the Pacific Northwest Electric Planning and Conservation Act passed by Congress in 1980. The act was the outgrowth of a plan proposed by PNUCC as a means of coordinating long-range power planning in the wake of the failure of the Hydro-Thermal Power Plan. The Council was given autonomy from any agency, public or private, and was to be funded by BPA. The Council's first chairman was former Washington governor Dan Evans, who was to lead the group of eight men, two from each state in the Northwest, to formulate a Regional Conservation and Electric Power Plan. It was widely hoped that the plan would be the blueprint for a solution to the WPPSS conundrum.

But the situation was rapidly becoming more complex. On September 29, 1982, the Springfield ratepayers won their suit when a Lane County Circuit Court judge ruled that 11 municipal utilities in Oregon had no legal authority to repay their share of the 4/5 debt. The ruling gave hope to Washington publics that they could get off the hook with regard to their own 4/5 commitments.

On November 5, the Idaho Supreme Court temporarily barred the towns of Heyburn and Burley from repaying their shares of the 4/5 debt. On December 15, Judge Joseph Coleman of King County Superior Court issued his first ruling in the Chemical Bank suit. He ruled that, if the Participants' Agreements were eventually found to be valid, Washington utilities would not have to pay more than their shares of the debt to make up for the shares owed by the remaining participants. The decision meant that Washington participants were not required to make up the 10 percent share of the 4/5 debt from utilities in Oregon and Idaho. It also meant that WPPSS was left with no way to repay the full amount of debt service on its outstanding 4/5 bonds.

On December 23, tiny Orcas Power & Light, a utility serving the San Juan islands, became the first 4/5 participant to file for federal bankruptcy protection. OPALCO's 0.006 percent share of the plants meant that it owed $45 million over the next 30 years, with $2.1 million due in 1983. The utility's chairman said that a 60 percent rate increase would have to go into effect immediately. OPALCO's financial dilemma was typical of the plight facing many of the 88 participants. Heyburn, Idaho, for example, with a miniscule share of the 4/5 debt, nevertheless owed $43,302 a month. With only 990 ratepayers, that meant that each ratepayer would have to pay $525 a year for the next 30 years on a project from which not one kilowatt would ever come. Such staggering prospects kept alive a flickering hope that Projects 4 and 5 could still be salvaged. Throughout 1982 and the first quarter of 1983, various 4/5 "rescue" plans were proposed, but the only one that seemed to have a fighting chance was a financing scheme concocted by former BPA Administrator Charles F. Luce.

Luce returned to Portland in 1982 after retiring as chairman of the board of Consolidated Edison, New York's major electric utility, where he had served since 1967 following a brief stint as undersecretary of the interior. Chuck Luce had a wide base of admirers in and out of the utility business; old hands at BPA and among the PUDs remembered the key role he had played in winning the Hanford generating plant for WPPSS. The Supply System was hoping that Luce could do it for them again, this time with 4 and 5. With WPPSS and the Big Four IOUs paying the consulting fees, Luce came up with a plan to save WNP-4 and 5, which he submitted to the Regional Council on January 3, 1983.

The plan called for creation of a nonprofit organization made up mostly of California utilities. The organization would obtain an option to purchase 4/5 from the 88 participants, and BPA would obtain an option to purchase the plants' output to meet regional demand. At first, the option purchases would provide enough money simply to preserve the plants' construction licenses and physical assets, an amount estimated at about $5 million a year. Eventually, as energy needs in California and the Northwest increased, the owner-consortium could pool the financing abilities of its member-utilities to begin construction on 4/5 again. Luce's report to the Council predicted that power from 4/5 would ultimately be needed in the Northwest, but marketing it to California in the form of long-term contracts would shift some of the costs to California utilities.

Council chairman Evans sensed that all eyes in the region were on the Council's treatment of 4/5 in the Regional Plan, and he did his best to play down the Council's role in the ultimate fate of the projects. "I do not believe it to be accurate or reasonable to lay at the feet of the Council blame for whether these plants rise or fail," he said. However, the truth was that the nonpartisan Regional Plan represented the only comprehensive formula that did not tread on the toes of one or two particular interest groups; more accurately, it was treading on everybody's toes equally. The regionwide consensus was the the projects would die for good if they were not included in the Council's plan.

On April 27, 1983, the Council released its Regional Plan, which included a list of "cost-effective options" to be pursued by utilities as the regional power situation warranted. WNP-4 and WNP-5 were not among the options. Evans, who had endorsed the plants seven years before, judged, along with the other Council members, that 4 and 5 were "the most expensive options in the region," and voted to drop any consideration of the projects from the final version of the plan. The decision effectively drove a stake into the hearts of WPPSS Nuclear Plants 4 and 5. Today, their massive concrete foundations (No. 4 was 18 percent complete and No. 5 15 percent when they were terminated) stand as the sole monuments to the ill-fated hydro-thermal program called Phase II.

But the clock had already been ticking on 4/5, and predictions of a default on the 4/5 bonds had seriously been considered since the end of 1982. On January 25, 1983, the 4/5 participants were supposed to begin paying interest to bondholders. All but two—Douglas County PUD in Washington and Wells Rural Cooperative in Nevada—ignored the payment deadline. The two payments totaled about $10,000, or 0.01 percent of the $93.9 million semiannual coupon payment owed to the bondholders.

On February 25, at BPA's recommendation, WPPSS ordered a construction slowdown on Project 3. Three days later, Standard & Poor's downgraded 4/5 to CC, its lowest rating for bonds not in default.

On May 13, Standard & Poor's suspended ratings for WNP-1, 2, and 3 bonds, virtually ensuring that WPPSS would not be able to sell more bonds until its financial situation improved. The same day, the WPPSS executive board ordered its staff to divert $24.7 million from the 4/5 accounts, a move widely interpreted as a first move toward default. The action was taken in order to cover probable administrative and legal fees that WPPSS could face should it default on 4/5 debts. Sequestering the funds left only about $3.3 million in the 4/5 account, not enough to pay even one month's interest, or $15.6 million. The due date for that payment into Chemical Bank's bond interest reserve fund passed on May 31. The bank issued a statement declaring that the failure to pay "constitutes a technical default. . . ."

The Supply System, numb from the swift succession of crisis after crisis, was nonetheless shocked on June 15, when the Washington State Supreme Court ruled that nine municipals and 20 PUDs in the state did not have the authority to execute the Participants' Agreements in 1976, making the contracts void from the beginning. The obligations of the 29 utilities represented 68.5 percent of the debt.

The ruling was completely unexpected because it reversed the decision of King County Superior Court. The state supreme court summarized its opinion as follows:

> The unconditional obligation to pay for no electricity is hardly the purchase of electricity. We hold that an agreement to purchase project capability does not qualify as purchase of electricity. . . .
>
> In the present case, the participants lacked substantive authority to enter into this type of contract because they constructed an elaborate financing agreement that required the participants to guarantee bond payments irrespective of whether the plant was ever completed; to surrender ownership interest and considerable control to WPPSS; and to assume the obligations of defaulting participants. As such, these contracts failed to protect unsuspecting individuals, the ratepayers, represented by the participants.

Chemical Bank was nonplussed by the Washington court's bombshell. The bank filed a motion asking the court to reconsider its decision, but there was little else to do; an appeal to a federal court was impossible because the Washington court had made its ruling on a state issue. The attorney for the co-ops shouldering the remainder of the 4/5 debt said that he would argue in the co-ops' ongoing King County case that the Participants' Agreements had changed in light of the state supreme court's ruling, and that therefore the co-ops should be absolved of the debt as well. Albert Malanca, the attorney for the victorious PUDs and municipals, said that he had approached Chemical Bank several times about a possible settlement, but that bank officials had refused to negotiate. Asked if the utilities planned to celebrate their triumph, Malanca said "You don't have a champagne celebration over a corpse."

The next day, Don Mazur, who had replaced the retiring Bob Ferguson as managing director on May 13, admitted that WPPSS was considering bankruptcy.

The next month was a frenzy of activity for the Supply System. Officials from WPPSS, the IOUs, BPA, and the Northwest's congressional delegation shuttled between Richland, New York, Seattle, and Washington, D.C., discussing every possible avenue for raising the funds needed to avoid default. Several of the region's representatives put together a bill to create a financing entity that would issue BPA-backed loans extended to the financially strapped Project 3.

On June 23, a small securities dealer in Santa Monica, California— Gibralco, Incorporated—became the first firm of its kind to fall victim to the WPPSS crisis. The firm had used WPPSS bonds as collateral on an $823,000 loan. After a drop in the value of the bonds in the wake of the Washington State Supreme Court decision, the bank that had issued the loan took over $797,000 in checking account balances from Gibralco, leaving the firm with a deficit of $258,297 and less than the minimum level of capital.

On June 28, it was disclosed that the Federal Bureau of Investigation and the Internal Revenue Service had been conducting a long-term investigation into the possibilities of kickbacks among contractors at WPPSS projects.

On June 30, another due date for the WPPSS $15.6 million monthly payment on 4/5 interest passed without Chemical Bank being paid.

On July 8, the executive board ordered that WNP-3 be mothballed for an indeterminate period. The chairman of WPPSS, Carl Halvorson, hung his head and bewailed the "disaster." But a much larger disaster was hovering very, very near, awaiting the inevitable signal for it to fall.

It was late in the afternoon, Friday, July 22, 1983. Attorneys for Chemical Bank and WPPSS were called into the Seattle courtroom of King County Superior Court Justice Joseph Coleman. Coleman informed the lawyers that he had just received word that the Washington State Supreme Court had refused to grant a request from Chemical Bank and WPPSS to reconsider its ruling which nullified the 4/5 contracts of 29 utilities. Therefore, Coleman announced that he was lifting the restraining order that he had issued on May 27, which had blocked Chemical Bank from declaring WPPSS in default of the 4/5 debt until after final disposition of the state supreme court.

Immediately, an attorney for Chemical Bank went to a pay phone to call Alexander Squire at WPPSS headquarters in Richland. Squire was the Supply System's financial director; the Chemical Bank attorney knew that an admission by Squire of WPPSS's inability to pay on the 4/5 debt would constitute a formal "event of default." With Squire on the end of the line, the lawyer asked:

"Do you admit that the Supply System does not have the ability to pay its bond obligations for WNP-4 and 5?"

The financial director for the Supply System replied, "Yes."

# 10

# FROM INSULT TO DEFAULT

It was the greatest financial disaster of its kind in history.

Bonds representing billions of dollars in investments were declared worthless. Half of those billions had come from loans extended simply to finance interest on debt, which the debtors refused to repay. Investors who, only a few months before, had bought into the utilities market on the promise of "no-risk guarantees of high returns" were left with little hope of ever seeing their ventures come to fruition. Fast-talking stockbrokers were blamed. Lawsuits were launched. Government investigations were initiated.

It was the summer of 1983. The public power crusade had come full circle since the collapse of Samuel Insull's utility holding company empire 51 years before. From out of the ashes of that empire had come a federal endorsement of public power, giving strength to the phenomenal growth of consumer-owned electricity in the Pacific Northwest. But the lessons that were learned in the wake of Insull's failure became lost over the years, so that by the time the ambitious nuclear program of the Washington Public Power Supply System had expanded to include five projects in 1976, few observers saw the danger of selling enormous amounts of securities backed by pieces of paper. In the 1920s, those pieces of paper were debentures signed by companies within Insull's corporate network which had no assets to speak of, only stocks from similar securities firms in the same network. In the 1970s, the documents that rendered value to WPPSS bonds for Projects 4 and 5 were the Participants' Agreements. When those agreements were ruled invalid in the courts, creditors had only the Supply System to turn to in order to pay a debt of almost $2.5 billion. In 1983, WPPSS assets consisted of the following: two complete power-generating facilities (Packwood Lake and Hanford) having a total output of about 877 megawatts; two terminated nuclear power projects (WNP-4 and 5), 15 percent and 18 percent complete; two deferred or "mothballed" nuclear power units (WNP-1 and 3), each about 60 percent complete; and one nuclear unit under construction (WNP-2), essentially complete and ready to be loaded with fuel.

In short, WPPSS had become a latter-day "paper pyramid," issuing billions of dollars in bonds which far exceeded in face value the total present worth of the agency. The public power crusade had ironically adopted the ways of one of its oldest and bitterest enemies, not only in its finances, but in its demeanor as well. It had grown distant from the ratepayers who owned it, just as the holding companies had become aloof to the wishes of their stockholders. The Supply System, originally so dedicated to the needs of its ratepayers, was in the end obsessed with its own survival, defensive against the tide of popular criticism, and belligerent toward the federal agency that had for many years treated it as the favorite son among the region's utilities. Embodied in the bloated bureaucracy of WPPSS, the crusade looked into the mirror and saw Insull.

Many conclusions have been drawn from the tragedy of the WPPSS default, and it is not my intention to review most of them, as they represent perspectives that are not enlightening in the context of this particular effort. However, as a means of bringing this first episode in the life of WPPSS (and the Supply System is still very much alive, in its own quiet and determined way) to a close, I will offer a few personal observations.

First, it is obvious that the Supply System was completely over its head in undertaking the construction of five nuclear units, particularly in light of its inexperience in dealing with the technology. True, WPPSS did build the Hanford generator, but that was a steam-generating system that utilized waste heat from a nuclear reactor that WPPSS did not build.

It should be noted that the problems of the WNP projects were reflected in nuclear power projects across the country during the 1970s and early 1980s. Some of these projects have suffered consequences even worse than those of WPPSS: Consolidated Edison's Byron 1 unit, for example, essentially completed at a cost of $3 billion, was denied an operating license by the Nuclear Regulatory Commission recently.

It may never be allowed to produce power. The Public Service Company of New Hampshire, meanwhile, is currently teetering on the brink of bankruptcy due to the soaring construction costs of the two Seabrook plants, of which it is the major sponsor. The crises of the Supply System have, to some extent, been the crises of the U.S. nuclear industry. WPPSS was only the first of many utilities that are reeling from the tremendous financial effects of their failed nuclear campaigns.

Nor was the Supply System's nuclear construction program the most ambitious in the country; the Tennessee Valley Authority had 17 nuclear units planned (14 were under construction) until quite recently. Today, two of those units are complete, four are still being built, and the rest have been cancelled.

Yet the WPPSS program had its unique qualities, and some of them worked to hasten events that led to default. The arrangements under which contractors were signed to work on the projects were wide open to the sorts of abuses that inevitably took place. The "change-order" system which characterized the early contracts was clumsy, but it at least acted as a check on quantum-leap cost increases; when it was done away with in 1975, the new "unpriced notice to proceed" was the equivalent of a "blank check" payable by the Supply System, as Stein discovered in 1976. The competitive-bid system for awarding contracts also had basic flaws, because it resulting in a plethora of contracts and contractors using a wide variety of equipment, technical processes, and management styles. One Supply System official explained the practice of hiring many contractors as the natural outcome of public power's "share the wealth" philosophy. Within the WPPSS nuclear power program that tradition evolved into a "give away the wealth" philosophy.

The Supply System did not, of course, operate in a vacuum, and it is not at all melodramatic to state that WPPSS was both villain and victim in the middle of a maelstrom of greed and apathy. The scene depicted by Gleckman is reminiscent of the scramble for securities in the booming market of the 1920s:

> From 1971, when WPPSS sold its first project notes, through 1980, Wall Street made tens of millions of dollars off the Supply System. Investment bankers and bond dealers became almost addicted to WPPSS bonds; with the vast supply and the attractive yields, there seemingly was no end to the underwriting fees and dealer markups. Few saw the mirror image of that picture: a market glut and a risky investment.

The cupidity of the financial community may have been matched by that of the contractors and their personnel at the WPPSS projects. Allegations from the current spate of lawsuits involving those projects paint a picture of racketerring on a level of that which colored Insull's Chicago. In one suit, the four largest electrical contractors in the country are accused of collusion for the purposes of fixing bids on contracts in Projects 1, 2, and 4.

Perhaps the greatest irony in the saga of the Supply System is that it represented both the greatest triumph of the public-power movement in the Northwest, and its cruelest blow. After three-quarters of a century of continual attacks on it by private utilities, the movement made peace with its enemies, only to discover that its new and greatest nemesis was its own ambition. There were no giants of the stature of J.D. Ross or Homer Bone to carry the banner of the crusade in the 1970s. The movers and shakers like Ken Billington and Nat Washington, masters at working behind the scenes to snatch an advantage for the crusade out of an apparent defeat, had retired by the time WPPSS began slipping into chaos. The crusade had run out of leaders by 1983, or perhaps they were simply lost in the fiscal and corporate maze of the Supply System, were as overwhelmed as J.D. Ross had been by the labyrinthine structure of Insull's pyramid.

In the aftermath of that government investigation of the utility holding companies that had so bewildered Ross, the advocates of a New Deal in the Pacific Northwest vowed that Insull's disaster must never happen again. In a radio address on January 17, 1938, Congressman Walter Pierce from Oregon warned that the "racketeers of Wall Street" must never be allowed to stand between publicly built power plants and those desiring to use those plants' power. "From a public-power viewpoint," said Pierce, "repetition of the 'paper pyramids' of the holding-company debacle with respect to electricity in the Northwest represents the unpardonable crime."

The paper pyramids of old have been replaced by towers of concrete and steel, standing useless and rusting in the rain above the forests of Satsop or gray and wind-beaten over the sagebrush of Hanford. The cooling towers from Projects 4 and 5 render the impression of permanence and strength, though they are actually static and lifeless. They are monoliths that have come to symbolize the Washington Public Power Supply System, built on the foundation of a sincere and determined belief in a better energy future for the Pacific Northwest through the benefits of public power. Today, the Supply System supplies some 2,000 megawatts to the region, about enough to meet 10 percent of the Northwest's energy needs. But the scope of the sweeping vision of WPPSS a few years ago has diminished. It is a vision brought back to reality after the illusions of power of the past.

# EPILOGUE

In July, 1984, WPPSS completed WNP-2's testing phase, and the plant began commercial operation.

WNP-1 and WNP-3, 63 percent and 76 percent complete, respectively, are still in a mothballed state at this writing. The Bonneville Power Administration is attempting to obtain a court ruling that would allow it to secure financing for completion of the units. The Supply System has been barred from the financial markets and carries a suspended credit rating in the wake of its $2.5-billion default.

Meanwhile, Bechtel Power Corporation has presented WPPSS with a plan for completing WNP-1 construction, either under a lump-sum or target price/incentive sharing arrangement.

The question remains whether the WPPSS plants will ever be needed. The Pacific Northwest is currently (1984) in the midst of a surplus of energy, which PNUCC's latest forecast has estimated will last for 10 years.

The most recent estimate of the total cost including interest of all five WPPSS projects is between $30 billion and $32 billion, regardless of whether WNP-1 and 3 ever be finished.

# BIBLIOGRAPHY

Bessey, Roy F. *Pacific Northwest Regional Planning—A Review*. Bulletin No. 6, Division of Power Resources, Department of Conservation. Olympia, WA: State Printing Plant, 1963.

Billington, Ken. Report to the board of directors of WPPSS, October 20, 1967.

————. "What *is* the PUD Past?" Address to annual convention of the Washington PUD Association, December 9, 1976.

————. "'WHUPS' or Will History Undo Public Skepticism?" Unpublished paper, March, 1982.

————. Interview with author, May, 1984.

Bonneville Power Administration. Department of Energy. *A Ten-Year Hydro-Thermal Power Program for the Pacific Northwest*. Portland, OR: BPA, 1969.

————. *Issue Backgrounder: BPA's Electric Power Rates*. Portland, OR: BPA, 1981.

Dick, Wesley Arden. "Visions of Abundance: The Public Power Crusade in the Pacific Northwest in the Era of J.D. Ross and the New Deal." Ph.D. dissertation, University of Washington, 1973.

Edinger, Vera. "The Hanford Story." Public relations release. Kennewick, WA: WPPSS, 1966.

Gleckman, Howard. "WPPSS: From Dream to Default." *Credit Markets* 1 (1984): 1, 53-64.

Hodel, Donald P. "The Prophets of Shortage." Address delivered to the City Club of Portland, July 11, 1975. Portland, OR: BPA, 1975.

Irish, Stephen L. Interview with author, January, 1984.

Lee, Kai N. and Donna Lee Klemka, with Marion E. Marts. *Electric Power and the Future of the Pacific Northwest*. Seattle: University of Washington Press, 1980.

McDonald, Forrest. *Insull*. Chicago: University of Chicago Press, 1962.

McKinley, Charles. *Uncle Sam in the Pacific Northwest*. Berkeley: University of California Press, 1952.

Northwest Power Planning Council. *Northwest Conservation and Electric Power Plan*. Portland, OR: The Council, 1983.

Norwood, Gus. *Columbia River Power for the People: A History of the Politics of the Bonneville Power Administration*. Portland, OR: BPA, 1981.

Nowakowski, Ragnar. Interview with author, January, 1984.

Olsen, Darryll. "The Washington Public Power Supply System: The Story So Far." *Public Utilities Fortnightly*, June 10, 1982, pp. 15-26.

Pacific Northwest Utilities Conference Committee. Long Range Projection of Loads and Resources 1977-78 through 1996-97, West Group Area. Portland, OR: PNUCC, April, 1977.

_____. Sum of Utilities Twenty-Year Forecast, 1983-2003, West Group Area. Portland, OR: PNUCC, June, 1983.

Pendergrass, Bonnie Baack. "Public Power, Politics, and Technology in the Eisenhower and Kennedy Years: The Hanford Dual-Purpose Reactor Controversy, 1956-1962." Ph.D. dissertation, University of Washington, 1974.

Perko, James R. Interview with author, January 1984.

Public Power Council. *Power Planning Primer*. Vancouver, WA: PPC, 1981.

Ramsay, M.L. *Pyramids of Power: The Story of Roosevelt, Insull, and the Utility Wars*. Indianapolis: Bobbs-Merrill, 1937.

Ross, J.D. *Science and Nature*. Seattle: University of Washington Press, 1932.

_____. "Seattle City Light and Power." *Public Ownership of Public Utilities* 16 (1934):83-92.

Sprague, Jennifer. "Washington's Low-Profile Power Planners." *Pacific Search* 7 (1977):16-18.

Springer, Vera. *Power and the Pacific Northwest*. Portland, OR: BPA, 1976.

Stein, J.J. Letter to Alvin Fletcher, January 4, 1977.

Thompson, Carl. *Confessions of the Power Trust*. New York: E.P. Dutton, 1932.

Washington Public Power Supply System. Minutes of meetings of the board of directors, 1957-1981.

_____. 1972 Status Report. Kennewick, WA: WPPSS, 1972.

_____. 1977 Status Report. Richland, WA: WPPSS, 1978.

_____. 1979 Status Report. Richland, WA: WPPSS, 1980.

_____. Biographical public relations releases, February 1979 and December 1981. Richland: WPPSS.

_____. "Meeting the Northwest's Energy Needs." Public relations release. Richland: WPPSS, 1983.

Welch, John. Interview with author, March 1984.

Periodicals and newspapers used as sources of information without bylines:

*Argus*
*Barron's*
*Bellingham Herald*
*Clearing Up*
*Credit Markets*
*Electrical World*
*Nuclear News*
*Nucleonics Week*
*Northwest Public Power Bulletin*
*Oregon Journal* (Portland)
*Oregonian* (Portland)
*Pacific Search*

*Public Power News*
*Public Utilities Fortnightly*
*Seattle Daily Journal of Commerce*
*Seattle Post-Intelligencer*
*Seattle Sun*
*Seattle Times*
*Tri-City Herald*
*Wall Street Journal*

# APPENDIX A

The power supply system of the Pacific Northwest has been founded on energy dissipated from falling water ever since the region's first electric generators were installed at a dam near Oregon City in 1884. In the century that has passed since then, other energy sources have played increasingly larger roles in the drive to meet the region's rising demands for electricity. Still, hydroelectric power today accounts for over 75 percent of the Northwest's generating capacity. Half of the total amount of power generated in the region comes from federal dams. This power is distributed by the Bonneville Power Administration.

The Bonneville Power Administration is a branch of the U.S. Department of Energy. It was established by Congress in 1937 to act as the marketing agent for power from Bonneville Dam, the first major dam built by the U.S. government on the Columbia River or its tributaries. When Grand Coulee Dam neared completion in 1941, BPA was also designated to market the power from this project.

Over the past 45 years, BPA assumed responsibility for marketing the power from 28 other federal dams in the Northwest. The dams have been built and operated by the U.S. Army Corps of Engineers and the Bureau of Reclamation. BPA does not build dams or power plants. However, as the principal distributor of regional power, BPA has designed and built the nation's largest network of long-distance, high-voltage transmission lines. The power features of the federal dams, together with the BPA's transmission system, are operated as a single unit known as the Federal Columbia River Power System.

BPA's service area includes that portion of the Columbia River drainage basin that lies within the United States. The full service area covers about 300,000 square miles and has a population of about 9 million. The BPA transmission network provides nearly 80 percent of the transmission capacity in the region. This network serves as the "backbone" grid for all interconnected utilities in the Northwest.

BPA wholesales power to 148 Northwest customers: 54 cooperatives, 37 municipalities, 26 public utility districts (PUDs), 15 industrial firms, 8 investor-owned utilities (IOUs), 6 federal agencies, the Washington Public Power Supply System (WPPSS), and an irrigation district.

The IOUs and some of the PUDs and municipals also own and operate power-generating facilities. The output from these non-federal facilities makes up the remaining 50 percent of the region's power capacity.

Northwest consumers have traditionally paid lower rates for their electricity than have ratepayers in all other parts of the Unites States. This tradition continues today.

The major reason for the Northwest's low rates has been the abundance of hydropower in the region. A secondary factor has been the heritage of intense competition between public and privately owned utilities. This inexpensive power contained hidden costs, however, which were not realized until five years ago. Prior to 1979, many homeowners, business owners, and farmers invested in equipment, such as space heaters, production machinery, and irrigation systems that use large amounts of electricity. There was little economic incentive to conserve; but dramatic increases in rates began in 1979. BPA's average rate to its direct-service industrial customers was even more severe, rising from 2 mills per kilowatt-hour to 24.5 mills per kilowatt-hour between 1965 and 1982, an increase of over 1,000 percent.

A major factor in the recent increases in BPA's rates has been the increased cost for nuclear plants 1, 2, and 3 being built by WPPSS.

A combination of rate hikes, an increased public interest in conservation, and a general economic slowdown has slackened growth substantially in the Northwest's demand for energy. Since 1941, electric loads grew at an annual rate of 6 to 7 percent. Since the early 1970s, this rate of growth has gradually declined to less than 1.5 percent per year.

Northwest electric loads once doubled in size every 10 to 12 years. At the present rate of growth, nearly 50 years will pass before the region's loads double again. As the development of hydropower resources has reached its limit, so has the general need for electricity.

# APPENDIX B

**1956**    *June 29*–The board of directors of the Washington PUD Association draws up a resolution calling on all publicly-owned utilities in the state to join in the formation of a joint operating agency, to be called the Washington Public Power Supply System.

*August 1*–A lawsuit is filed in Clallam County challenging the constitutionality of the state JOA law.

*September 7*–The JOA law is upheld in Clallam County Court. A few days later, the Washington Supreme Court adjudicates the legitimacy of WPPSS by concurring with the lower court.

*October 8*–Seventeen PUDs file an application with the Director of Conservation, seeking approval of their planned joint agency, WPPSS.

**1957**    Washington Director of Conservation Earl Coe signs an approval of WPPSS, thus officially establishing the agency.

*February 20*–The WPPSS board of directors holds its first meeting in Seattle.

*August 16*–Owen Hurd is selected as the first managing director of WPPSS.

*November 15*–The WPPSS main office is established in Kennewick.

**1958**    *September 26*–A permit for the Packwood Lake hydro project is granted to WPPSS by the FPC.

**1959**    *January*–The AEC requests PNUCC to review reports on the dual-purpose reactor proposed for Hanford. WPPSS is invited to participate in the review.

*July*–WPPSS proposes a joint public-private operation of the NPR.

**1960**    *March 15*–WPPSS files with the FPC for Nez Perce Dam on the Snake River.

**1960**   *March 16*–R. W. Beck & Associates submits a report to the AEC, which concludes that the NPR is technically and economically feasible.

**1961**   *April 29*–WPPSS files an amendment to its application for Nez Perce including PNPC's High Mountain Sheep Dam as a second-choice alternative.

*July 13*–The U.S. House of Representatives kills an amendment to the AEC authorization bill which would have included federal funds for conversion of the NPR to dual-purpose operation.

*September 22*–Washington Governor Rosellini requests the Department of Conservation to investigate the feasibility of the state undertaking installation of electrical generating facilities at Hanford.

*October 20*–The WPPSS Executive Committee authorizes assistance in non-federal construction of power facilities at Hanford and offers the services of WPPSS in financing construction of those facilities.

**1962**   *April 16*–BPA Administrator Luce discloses a plan for implementing the WPPSS proposal to an appropriations subcommittee of the House.

*July 6*–The General Accounting Office rules that Congressional approval must be obtained by the AEC before any contracts could be signed with WPPSS.

*July 17*–The House approves an amendment by Van Zandt prohibiting the use of Hanford steam to generate electricity.

*August 1*–The Senate approves a proposal that the AEC be allowed to sell steam to WPPSS.

*September 14*–The House votes against a Van Zandt motion to recommit a joint committee's recommendation of the Hanford Project.

*September 26*–Kennedy signs the Atomic Energy Commission Authorization Bill, including the Hanford Project.

**1963**   *May 8*–Bids are opened on the $122 million bond issue to finance the Hanford Generating Project—largest revenue bond issue at that time for the region.

*September 26*–Kennedy keynotes ground-breaking ceremonies for the HGP. Construction begins a few days later.

1964    *February 5*—The FPC issues a license to PNPC for the High
        Mountain Sheep Dam.

        *June*—The 27.5-MW Packwood Lake hydroelectric project,
        the first WPPSS power plant, is completed.

1966    *October*—At the behest of outgoing Bonneville Administra-
        tor Luce, new BPA chief David Black convenes the first
        meeting of the Joint Power Planning Council in Portland.

        *November*—The HGP begins commercial operation.

        The Public Power Council is formed as the power-planning
        arm of the region's publicly owned utilities.

1967    *April*—WPPSS sends a report to the PPC and BPA, propos-
        ing construction of a nuclear power plant by WPPSS, in
        order to meet regional needs.

        *June 5*—The U.S. Supreme Court rules that the FPC should
        reconsider its licensing of the PNPC project.

        *September 28*—WPPSS and PNPC announce agreement on
        a joint effort to build High Mountain Sheep Dam.

1968    *December*—The JPPC announces its ten-year Hydro-Ther-
        mal Power Program, which aims to build five nuclear units
        and two coal-fired plants by 1979, at a total cost of $2
        billion.

1969    *January*—A PPC plan, representing the participation of
        public utilities in the HTPP, calls for EWEB to build a major
        nuclear plant in Oregon by late 1974. The plan designates
        WPPSS as the sponsor of a nuclear plant to be completed
        in 1975.

1970    *May 26*—The sponsorship of public power's first nuclear
        plant is transferred to WPPSS as a result of a referendum in
        Eugene which effectively halts EWEB's power-plant siting
        studies.

        *July 17*—The WPPSS board of directors authorizes applica-
        tion to the AEC for a construction permit for the purpose
        of building a nuclear plant on the central Washington coast
        by 1977.

        *October 14*—WPPSS restructures its management and
        changes the site of its nuclear project to Hanford, dubbing
        the project Hanford No. 2.

**1971**    *January 5*—WPPSS signs net-billing contracts with BPA to guarantee $15 million in interim financing for beginning construction of No. 2.

*January 27*—WPPSS Managing Director Hurd receives a directive from the White House to permanently shut down the N-reactor at Hanford, in compliance with the presidential budget.

*January 28*—Governor Evans and Senator Jackson announce that they will go to Washington, D.C. to fight the shutdown of the N-reactor.

*March 31*—The AEC agrees to continue to operate the N-reactor for 3 more years, at a cost to WPPSS of $20 million a year. WPPSS is given 15 months to decide whether it will assume responsibility of operating the reactor.

**1972**    *May*—WPPSS proposes adding a high-pressure topping turbine to the Hanford generator, while simultaneously building a new reactor. The PPC assents to the plan, and also asks WPPSS to build a complete nuclear power plant in western Washington, later called WNP-3.

*September*—WPPSS revises its plan for Hanford. Instead of building a reactor alone, WPPSS plans to design a complete nuclear power plant (WNP-1), to be constructed near No. 2, already under construction.

Stein becomes the new WPPSS managing director following Hurd's retirement.

**1973**    *January*—BPA Administrator Hodel calls on regional power planners to revise the floundering Hydro-Thermal Power Program.

*August*—WPPSS authorizes construction of a $2.5 million headquarters building in Richland.

*October*—An oil embargo by Arab oil-exporting countries brings about a national awareness of an "energy crisis."

*December 14*—Hodel announces plans for "Phase II" of the HTPP, which includes construction of WNP-4 and WNP-5 by WPPSS.

**1974**    *February*—Site hearings begin for WNP-3 at Satsop.

*March*—Strikes at Projects 1 and 2 delay construction for several weeks.

**1974**  *May 29*—WPPSS agrees to build WNP-4 and WNP-5 as "twins" of units 1 and 3.

**1976**  *January*—WPPSS fires the constructor of WNP-2, which is two years behind schedule.

*April 11*—WPPSS tests of water intake mechanisms at WNP-1 kill millions of salmon fry in the Columbia.

*June 16*—Hodel issues a notice of power insufficiency to all BPA customers, informing them that BPA could not guarantee to meet their power needs beyond 1982. The issuance of the notice persuades enough public utilities to sign the controversial Participants' Agreements to meet the required number of ownership shares (88).

*October*—The Satsop site for WNP-3/5 is certified by the state.

**1977**  *March*—Strand is made the new managing director of WPPSS upon Stein's retirement.

*May*—Site clearing begins at Satsop.

*June*—WPPSS begins to assume management of WNP-2 from Burns & Roe.

*November 17*—Strand issues a stop-work order for 3/5 due to severe erosion caused by heavy rains at the Satsop site.

**1978**  *June 24-25*—The Crabshell Alliance holds a "reclamation" demonstration at Satsop. Despite 156 arrests, the demonstration is generally peaceful.

*July*—The Crabshell Alliance files the first class-action suit against WPPSS, challenging its construction program.

BPA hires Theodore Barry & Associates to do an independent management study of WPPSS.

WPPSS informs the PPC that it is studying the capability of WPPSS to build more power plants. The PPC advises that the study be postponed.

*October 5*—The Seattle *Post-Intelligencer* reveals that 135 faulty welds have been found at WNP-2. A WPPSS spokesman says that the quality-control division was "deficient" at the time the welds were made, and adds: "We have since beefed up quality control, and if that were to occur today, the defective welds would be caught quickly."

**1978** *December 5*—WPPSS staffers submit to the board of directors a regional electric plan proposing that WPPSS replace BPA as the power supplier for all the public utilities in the region. The plan also would hold all low-cost federal hydropower for the exclusive use of public utility customers. Strand says that he authorized preparation of the program in order to assure bondholders that, should regional energy legislation fail to pass in Congress, the region's power supply system would not "fall into chaos."

**1979** *January 5*—The Barry report cites a need for improved management at WPPSS, and for a stronger overseer's role by BPA in Supply System affairs.

*March 27*—A Hanford scientist petitions the Richland city council to ask WPPSS to fire Strand.

*March 29*—An accident at the Three Mile Island nuclear power facility in Pennsylvania sparks a fresh controversy over the safety of nuclear power.

*July*—The NRC fines WPPSS $60,000 for "construction inadequacies" at WNP-2. The agency reports that, in the course of its inspection of the plant preceding the Supply System's planned final tests, over 20,000 defective welds were found. WPPSS does not contest the fine. Subsequent repairs to the plant set the commercial operation date 15 months later than planned.

**1980** *February 8*—Strand is fired.

*May*—The WPPSS construction budget is estimated at $16 billion, an increase of nearly 50 percent over the previous year's estimate of $11 billion.

*June*—Ferguson is named new managing director.

**1981** *May 29*—Ferguson announces to the board of directors that a "bottoms up" review of the WPPSS construction budget indicates a probable total cost of $24 billion for all five plants. He recommends a one-year moratorium on construction on WNP-4 and WNP-5.

*June*—The PNUCC ten-year forecast for Northwest power loads reflects the considerable decline in regional electricity demands, and estimates that the output from WNP 4/5 will not be needed until 1988.

**1981**     *November*—Initiative 394, which forbids bond sales by WPPSS after June 1982, unless approved by the state's voters, is overwhelmingly passed in Washington state.

*December 26*—Ratepayers in Springfield, Oregon, sue their municipal utility in order to keep it from paying its share of the 4/5 debt.

**1982**     *January 5*—Clark County PUD refuses to help WPPSS finance a construction halt on 4/5.

*January 6*—Moody's suspends its rating on 4/5.

*January 16*—A committee representing the 88 utilities participating in the 4/5 projects fails to come to an agreement on how to finance a construction moratorium on the two projects.

*January 20*—Ferguson recommends cancellation of 4/5.

*January 22*—The WPPSS directors vote to terminate 4/5.

*January 23*—The WPPSS work force, including contracted employees, begins to decline from its peak of nearly 24,000 as layoffs begin from the cancelled 4/5 programs.

*March*—Two thousand ratepayers converge on the offices of Snohomish County PUD in Everett to protest the WPPSS record bond issue of $850 million.

*April*—Six thousand people march from downtown Richland to WPPSS headquarters in support of continued construction of WNP-1. Under pressure from BPA, however, the WPPSS directors vote for a construction moratorium on the project to last up to 5 years.

Initiative 394 is declared unconstitutional by the Washington State Supreme Court.

*May 18*—On behalf of 4/5 bondholders, Chemical Bank files suit against the 88 participants in 4/5.

*September 29*—A Lane County Circuit judge frees 11 Oregon municipal utilities from their shares of the 4/5 debt by ruling that they had no legal authority to sign the Participants' Agreements.

*November 15*—Eleven Washington PUDs file suit in U.S. Claims Court against the federal government, claiming that BPA had "coerced" them into backing construction of 4/5.

**1983**  *January 25*—Interest on the 4/5 debt comes due, but only 2 of the 88 participating utilities pay.

*January 26*—Chemical Bank, on behalf of the 4/5 bond holders, files suit in U.S. District Court in Portland against Oregon utilities that signed the Participants' Agreements in 1976.

*April 27*—The Regional Power Planning Council adopts its Conservation and Electric Power Plan for the Northwest's energy future. No mention of WNP 4/5 is made anywhere in the plan, effectively sealing the plants' termination once and for all.

*May 13*—Standard & Poor's suspends ratings for bonds for remaining WPPSS projects, virtually ensuring that the Supply System cannot sell any more bonds without a radical turnaround in its financial condition.

*May 27*—The WPPSS executive board votes to begin a three-year mothballing of WNP-3. The four IOUs holding 30 percent ownership of the project threaten legal action if WPPSS mothballs the plant.

King County Superior Court Justice Joseph Coleman issues a restraining order against any attempt by Chemical Bank to declare a default on 4/5 bonds, pending judgment on responsibility for the debt.

*May 31*—The due date for the $15.6 million monthly WPPSS payment into Chemical Bank's bond interest reserve fund passes with WPPSS unable to pay. Chemical Bank issues a statement declaring that failure to pay "constitutes a technical default."

*June 15*—The Washington State Supreme Court rules that nine municipals and 20 PUDs in Washington did not have authority to execute the 4/5 Participants' Agreements, rendering the contracts void from the beginning.

*June 23-24*—The WPPSS executive board meets for two days in Seattle to discuss the impending crisis, but no clear plan materializes.

*July 14*—The chief executive officers of the "Big Four" Northwest IOUs, along with representatives from Seattle City Light, BPA, and the DSIs, meet with four Northwest Senators in Washington, D.C., in order to discuss legislation that will assist WPPSS in resuming work on WNP-3.

**1983**     *July 22*–Coleman lifts the restraining order he issued on May 27, prompting Chemical Bank to declare WPPSS in default of the 4/5 debt. WPPSS admits to Chemical Bank's attorneys that it is unable to pay its bond obligations, but withholds public announcement of the default until the following Monday, July 25. The amount defaulted, $2.5 billion, constitutes the largest municipal default in history.

# INDEX

AFL-CIO, 80
Allen, Frederick Lewis, 16
Aluminum Company of America, 30
Appropriations Committee, 75
Arab oil embargo, 95
Army Corps of Engineers, 28, 39
atomic bomb, development of, 50-51
Atomic Energy Commission (AEC),
    51, 52, 53, 54, 55, 64, 66, 81,
    83, 95; authorization bill, 60,
    65; NPR plan and, 61, 62
atomic plant: first commercial, 52;
    second commercial, 99
Austen, Eileen, 125

Baker, Martin, 114
Banking and Commerce, Senate
    Committee on, 16
Barline, Dean, 33
*Barron's*, 60
Bechtel Corporation, 122
Beck, Robert W., 24, 48, 57, 58
*Bellingham Herald*, 115, 116
Big Four IOUs, 93, 130; coal-fired
    thermal plant and, 73
Bellington, Ken, 21, 24-28, 35, 36,
    43, 46; 4/5 contracts and, 69,
    74, 76, 77; future course of PUD
    affairs, 32-33; nuclear program
    and, 48, 49, 55, 60, 63, 64, 65;
    as officer in NHCA, 40, 41
Black, David S., 68, 70, 71
Black Thursday, 6
bonds: general lien, 23; municipal,
    23; revenue, 23, 24
Bone, Homer Truitt, 2, 10, 11, 12,
    14, 15, 25
Bone Bill, 10

Bonneville Power Administration
    (BPA), 21-37, 79, 85, 86, 88,
    91, 92, 94, 105, 125, 129, 132;
    birth of WPPSS and, 39, 43, 44,
    46; financing of Hanford No. 2
    plant and, 84; 4/5 contracts and,
    66, 70, 72, 74, 75, 76, 130, 131;
    Lawyers Relief Act and, 117,
    118, 120, 121; nuclear program
    and, 55, 56, 61, 62
Bonneville Project Act, 29
Bovers, Charles, 80
Bray, Lane, 103
brownouts, 32
Bureau of Reclamation, 39
Bureau of the Budget, 60

Caples, Elwood, 25
Chamberlain, Fred, 24
Chemical Bank (New York), 128,
    131, 132, 133
Church, Frank, 45
Civic Opera House (Chicago), 6
Clagett, Fred, 115
Cleveland, Vincent, 40
Cluck, Jack, 23, 48, 49, 73, 74
Coalition for Safe Power, 99
Coe, Earl, 48, 49, 60, 61
Coleman, Joseph, 129, 133
Columbia River power sources, 7;
    Priest Rapids Dam, 35
Commonwealth Edison, 3
Commonwealth Electric Company, 3
*Congressional Record*, 63
Conservation, State Department of,
    36, 61, 68
Consolidated Edison Company, 52,
    130

Construction Impact Group, 103, 104
Cooke, Morris, 12
Coon, Sam, 45
Court of Appeals, U.S., 44
Crabshell Alliance, 116, 126
Crusade for Public Power, 21

Dam, Joseph, 41
Davis, Harvey, 33
Davis, Joe, 77
Davis, Ralph, 77
Defense Electricity Production Act, 39
Defense Power Administration (DEPA), 32, 33
direct-service industry (DSI), 30, 88, 89, 92
Dixon-Yates private utility syndicate, 43
Dixon-Yates scandal, 44
Douglas, William O., 18
Douglas United Nuclear, 80
Drexel Burnham Lambert Incorporated, 125
Duquesne Light & Power Company, 52
Duree, Jim, 117
Du Vall, George, 116

Eastman, Blyth, 91
Edison, Thomas Alva, 2, 9
Edison Electric Institute, 39
Edwards, Frank, 12
Ehrlichman, John, 79, 80
Eisenhower, Dwight, 43
Eisenhower Administration, 38, 40
electric power, monopolization of, 22
Elizabeth, Queen of England, 53
Ellsworth, Harrison, 45
eminent domain, 23
Energy, Department of, 122
*Energy 1990*, 114

energy crisis, 95
Energy Facility Siting Evaluation Committee (EFSEC), 103, 115, 116
environmental groups, 114
environmental impact statement (EIS), 92
Eugene Water and Electric Board (EWEB), 82, 83, 99
Evans, Dan, 81, 94, 129, 130, 131

Farmer-Labor party, 10
Federal Bureau of Investigation (FBI), 133
Federal Power Act, 59, 68
Federal Power Commission (FPC), 18, 46, 55, 57, 59, 60, 63; construction of Priest Rapids Dam and, 35, 40, 41; dam at Oxbow, 39; 4/5 contracts and, 68, 69, 70; Middle Snake dams, 44, 47
Federal Trade Commission (FTC), 4, 10, 42
Ferguson, Robert L., 122, 124, 125, 127, 132
financial collapse, 1-2
Fischer, Ed. 76, 77, 101, 106
Fisheries, State Department of, 103
fish kill incident, 103
Ford, Henry, 5
Frisbee, Donald, 77

Galbraith, W. A., 44
General Accounting Office (GAO), 62, 75
General Electric, 17, 51, 53, 106
generating station, first electrical, 2
Gleckman, Howard, 123, 126
Goldhammer, Bernard, 75
Goldsbury, John, 119, 120
Greimes, Grover, 43

Halvorson, Carl, 133
Hanford Atomic Works, 50, 106

Hanford Generating Project (HGP), 66, 81, 96, 97; key benefits, 62; lobbying efforts, 64
Hanford military reservation, 66
Hatfield, Mark, 63
Healy, Robert, 6
Hodel, Don, 87, 88, 91, 92, 93, 99, 118
holding companies, 2
Holifield, Chet, 63
Hoover, Herbert, 7
Hosmer, Craig, 60, 64, 65
House Appropriations Committee, 31
House Interior Committee, 46
House of Insull, 1
House of Morgan, 1
Hulbert, William G., 83, 119
Hurd, Owen, 40, 46, 54, 60, 63, 65, 79, 80, 82, 86; 4/5 contracts, 69; managing director for WPPSS, 49-50, 55
Hydro-Thermal Power Program (HTPP), 74, 75, 76, 77, 82, 93, 94, 99, 103, 114, 118, 129; costs, 86, 87; net billing, 88, 89; N-reactor shut down threat, 81

Ickes, Harold, 14, 18, 23, 29
Idaho Power Company (IPCO), 39, 40, 41, 44, 45, 46
Illinois Commerce Commission, 29
Insull, Martin, 4, 16, 17
Insull, Samuel, 1, 2, 6, 7, 16, 17, 20, 29; expanded control of utilities, 4
Insull Utility Investments, Inc., 3
Interior, Department of, 68, 118; Office of Audit, 117
Internal Revenue Service (IRS), 133
investor-owned utility (IOU), 23, 29, 30-33, 67, 73, 77, 85, 87, 89, 92, 103, 132; birth of WPPSS and, 39, 41, 42, 46; capital

[investor-owned utility (IOU)] financing and, 71, 72; consumer viewpoint of, 98; nuclear program and, 56, 63, 64

Jackson, Henry, 44, 51, 53, 63, 64, 69, 80
Jensen, Ben, 32
Johnson, Peter, 126
Joint Committee on Atomic Energy (JCAE), 51, 53, 57, 60, 63, 64
joint operating agency (JOA), 33, 34, 35, 36, 43, 44, 49, 55, 76
Joint Power Planning Committee (JPPC), 70, 71, 72, 74, 81, 82
Joseph, George, 11, 15
Juggernaut, 69, 78

Keeting, R. L., 43
Kennedy, John F., 60, 66
Kings County Superior Court, 132
Korean War, 32

labor disputes, 97, 104
Langlie, Arthur B., 34, 41, 44, 45
Langlie Administration, 49
Lawyer's Relief Act of 1982, 128
Lee, Kai, 100
Lewis, Nick, 115
Liberty bonds, 3
license issuing, 41, 46, 59, 68
Luce, Charles F., 62, 69, 70, 87, 130

McCall, Tom, 82
McCarthyism, 38
McGelwee, Frank, 117
McKay, Douglas, 45, 46
McKee, Paul, 46
Magnusson, Warren G., 44, 45, 120
Malanca, Albert, 132
Manhattan Project, 50
Mazur, Don, 132
Meany, George, 80
media manipulation, 5-6

Middle West Utilities Company, 3
Montana Power, 41
Morse, Wayne, 44, 45
Morton, Rogers, 94
Mountain States Power, 41
Munro, Sterling, 118, 119, 120
Murphy, Malachy, 115
Muscle Shoals, 5, 7
Myers, Guy, 23

National Electric Light Association
    (NELA), 4, 5, 10, 15, 39, 43
National Hells Canyon Association
    (NHCA), 40, 41, 44, 46
Natural Resources Defense Council,
    92
Nelson, Lars, 48, 77
Neuberger, Richard, 44
New Deal, 31, 38
New Deal mandate, 25
new production reactor (NPR), 55,
    56, 57, 61, 63, 64, 65, 66, 67
New York Power Authority (NYPA),
    7, 12
Nez Perce Dam, 57-59
Nixon, Richard, 57
Nixon administration, 80, 81
Norris, George W., 5
Northwest Energy Company, 31
Northwest Power Pool (NWPP), 30,
    39, 56
Northwest Public Power Association
    (NWPPA), 27, 32, 40, 85, 92
Northwestern University, 29
nuclear age, 65
nuclear boom, 96
Nuclear Moratorium Initiative, 99
nuclear power: commercial, 86; op-
    position to, 99; support for, 92
nuclear power plant, consumer-
    owned, 79
nuclear program, 48-65; research
    costs, 52; science-oriented com-
    mittees, 53

Nuclear Regulatory Commission, 108
Nuclear Safeguards Act, 99

Office of Management and Budget
    (OMB), 75, 80, 84
open-ended financing, 105
Orcas Power and Light (OPALCO),
    129

Pacific Northwest Electric Planning
    and Conservation Act (1980),
    129
Pacific Northwest Power Company
    (PNPC), 41, 46, 47, 52, 57, 58,
    59, 60, 67, 68, 69
Pacific Northwest Regional Planning
    Commission (PNWRPC), 18, 19
Pacific Northwest Utilities Confer-
    ence Committee (PNUCC), 56,
    70, 88, 91, 94, 128
Pacific Power & Light Company
    (PP&L), 31, 41, 46, 73, 77, 98,
    128
Packwood Lake hydroelectric plant,
    67
Packwood Lake power project, 55,
    59
partnership policy, 39, 41
Pastore, John, 54
Patterson, Donald, 91
Pebble Springs nuclear plants, 128
Pebble Springs project, 99
People's Utility District (PUD),
    Oregon, 11, 22. *See also* Public
    Utility District (PUD), Wash-
    ington
Pinchot, Gifford, 5
pipefitter's strike, 104
plutonium, 100
plutonium reactor, convertible type,
    55
*Port of Astoria* v. *Hodel*, 92
Portland General Electric Company
    (PGE), 41, 73, 82, 99, 128

power facilities, government-owned vs. private enterprise, 5-6
power insufficiency, notice of, 93
power planning, regional, beginning of, 1-20
power shortages, 32
power surpluses, 31
Power Trust, 2, 5, 9, 10, 11, 12, 15, 20, 23; regulation of, 14
private utilities, condemnations suits against, 23
prophets of shortage, 92
Public Ownership League, 26
public power, debate over, 5
Public Power Council (PPC), 72, 82, 83, 84, 85, 90, 96, 114
public-power districts, 11
public-power fortresses, 22
Public Power League, 27
public-power movement, 2, 10, 12
Public Service Company of Northern Illinois, 3
Public Utility District (PUD), Washington, 11, 21, 22, 23, 25-37, 40, 42, 46, 56, 64; as financial consultants, 24; JOA and, 43-44; partnership policies, 39, 41; Snohomish County, 54; WPPSS and, 48-50, 54, 55, 58. *See also* Peoples Utility District (PUD), Oregon
Public Utility Holding Company Act (1935), 18
Public Works Administration (PWA), 18, 23
Puget Sound Power & Light Company (PSP&L), 9, 10, 12, 27, 31, 33, 86, 115, 128; 4/5 contracts, 73, 76, 77
Puget Sound Utilities Council, 71
Puget Sound-Willamette Valley corridor, 85
pyramiding, 3, 17

Quast, Tom, 54

Radin, Alex, 58, 64
rainfall effect on site construction, 108-113
Raver, Paul J., 29, 30, 31, 32, 39, 56
*Reader's Digest*, 39
Regional Power Planning Council, 129
Rice, Donald B., 81
Richmond, H. R., 76, 87
Ross, James Delmadge, 8, 14, 15, 18, 20, 23, 25, 29, 42; firing of, 12
Roosevelt, Franklin Delano, 7, 13; issue of public power and, 7, 13-15
Roselline, Albert D., 61, 63, 65, 66

Satre, Wendall, 77
Seaborg, Glenn T., 61
Seaton, Fred, 46
Seattle City Light (SCL), 8, 9, 10, 12, 23, 84, 101
Seattle *Post-Intelligencer*, 12, 117, 121, 126
Secretary Of The Interior, 60, 89
securities, worthless, 1, 134
Securities and Exchange Commission (SEC), 18, 19
Senate Committee on Banking and Commerce, 16
shotrock, 108, 113
Smyth, Henery de Wolf, 53
socialism, 38
Springfield Utility Board, 127
Sputnik satellite, 53
Squire, Alexander, 133
Standard & Poor's, 123, 125, 131
standpatters, 12
State Power Commission (SPC), 34, 35, 36, 49
Stein, J. J., 54, 86, 87, 97, 98, 105, 106

stock market crash (1929), 6
Strand, Neil, 105, 106, 107, 116, 118, 121, 122
Strauss, Lewis, 52, 53
Supreme Court: U.S., 46, 68; Washington State, 131, 133
Swidler, Joseph C., 68

Taylor, Ed, 76, 77, 81
Tennessee Valley Authority (TVA), 24, 28, 43, 72
Treasury, U.S., 28
*Tri-City Herald*, 65, 80, 102

Udall, Stewart, 68
Ullman, Al, 45
utilities, consolidation of, 3

Van Zandt, James, 60, 63, 64
Vickery, Gordon, 101, 114

Wagenhoffer, Tom, 118
Walkley, Glenn, 54, 104, 119
*Wall Street Journal*, 60, 61
War Production Board, 30
Ward, Frank, 49
Washington Environmental Council, 114
Washington Public Power Supply System (WPPSS), 37, 95-98, 101-113, 115, 122, 132, 133, 134; Barry report, 119-120;

[Washington Public Power Supply System (WPPSS)]
bonds, 123, 133; bond sale, 124, 125; Crabshell Alliance and, 116; first resolutions, 48; formation of, 38-47; 4/5 contracts, 66-78; Lawyers' Relief Act of 1982 and, 128; NPR troubles and, 79-95; nuclear program and, 48-65; ratepayers and, 126, 127; Snohomish withdrawal from, 54
Washington Public Utilities Districts Association, 21
Washington State Power Commission, 41
Washington Water Power Company (WWP), 31, 41, 73, 77
Weinberger, Caspar, 80
Wells Rural Cooperative, 131
Welker, Herman, 45
*Weltanschauuing*, 101
WNP bonds, 123
WNP projects, 120
World War I, 3
World War II, 29
"WPPSS: From Dream to Default," 123

Yom Kippur War, 95
Young, Owen D., 17

Zaharoff, Basil, 16

# ABOUT THE AUTHOR

**D. Victor Anderson** is an economic consultant with the Energy Research Group, Inc. of Portland, Oregon. Until 1984 he was a resources analyst with the Pacific Northwest Utilities Conference Committee in Portland.

Mr. Anderson coordinated the compilation of the Northwest's first comprehensive thermal resources database, one of PNUCC's most widely circulated reports. He is currently working on a reference book of major nuclear power plant projects.

He holds a B.A. in political science from the University of Oregon, Eugene, and an M.A. in development economics from the University of Denver, Denver, Colorado.